*Appraisal and
Professional Development
in the Primary School*

Appraisal and Professional Development in the Primary School

CHRISTOPHER DAY,
PATRICK WHITAKER
AND DAVID WREN

OPEN UNIVERSITY PRESS
MILTON KEYNES · PHILADELPHIA

Open University Press
Open University Educational Enterprises Limited
12 Cofferidge Close
Stony Stratford
Milton Keynes MK11 1BY

and
242 Cherry Street
Philadelphia, PA 19106, USA

First published 1987

Copyright © Christopher Day, Patrick Whitaker, David Wren 1987

All rights reserved. No part of this publication may be
reproduced, stored in a retrieval system or transmitted in
any form or by any means, without written permission from the
publisher.

British Library Cataloguing in Publication Data
Day, Christopher
  Appraisal and professional development
  in primary schools.
  1. Elementary school teachers—Great
  Britain—Rating of
  I. Title II. Whitaker, Patrick
  III. Wren, David
  372.11'44'0941   LB2838

ISBN 0-335-15542-1
ISBN 0-335-15541-3 Pbk

Library of Congress Cataloging in Publication Data
Day, Christopher, A.C.P.
  Appraisal and professional development
  in primary schools.
  Bibliography: P.
  Includes index.
  1. Elementary school teachers—Great
  Britain—Rating of.
  2. School supervision, elementary—Great Britain.
  3. Elementary school teachers—
  Great Britain. I. Whitaker, Patrick.
  II. Wren, David (David C.) III. Title
  LB2838.D33   1987   372.11'44'0941   87-24797

ISBN 0-335-15542-1
ISBN 0-335-15541-3 (pbk.)

Typeset by GCS, Leighton Buzzard
Printed in Great Britain by The Alden Press, Oxford

Contents

List of figures and tables	vii
Foreword	ix
Notes on the authors	xi
1 The context of appraisal and professional development	1
2 Teacher learning and change	13
3 The organisational setting	32
4 Teacher and school review	52
5 Inquiring into classroom action	79
6 The appraisal interview	114
7 Personal and professional relationships	125
8 Building a school policy	147
Bibliography	161
Index	168

Figures and tables

Figures

2.1	An interventionist model for promoting professional development	29
3.1	The organisational model	35
4.1	The five stages of the institutional review and development process	58
4.2	DION problem-solving process	60
4.3	The teacher's self-evaluation	63
4.4	The headteachers's self-evaluation	64
4.5	The action research spiral	67
4.6	Action research as a spiral staircase	69
5.1	Classroom observation: a sequence of activities	88
5.2	Focuses for classroom inquiry	89
5.3	The use of classroom data	91
5.4	Checking whether an inference is soundly based on evidence, or unsubstantiated	91
5.5	Triangulation as a means of validating interpretations of classrooms	92
5.6	Five phases of reporting	93
5.7	A representation of the processing of descriptive data	96
5.8	Infant teacher classroom speech schedule	104
5.9	An example of instant coding of 3 minutes of teacher talk	104
5.10	Classroom talk audiences	105
5.11	Understanding versus Judging	107
5.12	Action checklist for aggressive behaviour	107
7.1	The skills of active listening	132
7.2	The Jo-Hari Window	138
7.3	Factors relating to human growth and development	145
8.1	Hierarchical structure	149
8.2	Collegial structure	150
8.3	A model for building a school appraisal and professional development policy	152

Tables

4.1	Planning evaluation in your school	61
4.2	Conditions for successful appraisal	62
5.1	Approaches to classroom enquiry	82
5.2	Lesson profile	97
5.3	Teaching organisation, pupil roles, and teacher-pupil relationships	98
5.4	Pupil pursuit	100
6.1	Appraisal comment form and summary sheet	120
7.1	Giving feedback	139

Foreword

This book has been written out of belief that the ultimate responsibility for the quality of education which our children actually receive in schools will always rest with teachers. Governments, local education authorities and others may legislate, create and manage policy, monitor and attempt to influence the curriculum and its delivery through research, writing and professional development opportunities. In the end, however, it will be groups of teachers in their schools and individual teachers in their classrooms who will, either because of or in spite of external initiatives, help children to realise their potential. Any development of teacher and school appraisal must, therefore, take into account the social, economic, political and organisational contexts in which teachers work and the practical, personal and interpersonal factors which will inevitably affect their attitudes.

If appraisal is to be seen as part of every teacher's professional development then appraisal systems must take into account how teachers may learn most effectively and provide conditions which will support this learning and any changes which result. For if appraisal is to be judged by teachers and others as worthwhile it must have positive and practical outcomes. It must be perceived as having benefits for pupils, teachers and the community at large. Investments must be made not only in the design and implementation of appraisal in schools, but also in support for its outcomes. Professional development and institutional needs which will be identified as a result of appraisal processes must be met or it will come to be perceived as yet another management exercise imposed for the sole purpose of external accountability.

In this book we take the view that appraisal and professional development are complex and delicate processes in which careful consideration needs to be made of a number of organisational, personal and interpersonal factors. Teachers' learning will, for example, be affected by psychological and organisational constraints and governed by opportunities for reflection and self-confrontation which themselves require the support and empathy of critical friends. Whilst self-appraisal is likely, for practical if not professional reasons, to be the key-stone of any appraisal system, not all teachers will necessarily have acquired the means or the skills to achieve this, particularly where it involves systematic classroom inquiry. Inevitably in the day to day business of classroom life most teachers work at an intuitive level. If they are to participate in formal appraisal schemes they will need to move to more consciously reflective modes of operation. They are likely to spend more time in disclosure to and feedback from colleagues through informal and formal changes. This will require skills in, for example, consultation and negotiation, active listening, attending, empathy and even counselling.

Those in schools with management responsibilities will need to ensure that the organisational climate is supportive, that interpersonal relationships are strong, that there is a sense of individual and collective worth. They must invest time and resources in the act of appraisal and professional development. They must be able to ensure, through their management practices, that appraisal is perceived as an opportunity for further professional growth rather than a threat to professional status. They must also be able to provide practical support, for example in needs identification and classroom and school review through school policies which promote clear agreements of roles and responsibilities. They must promote collegiality as a criteria for development.

We attempt in this book to offer our own thoughts and those of others on these and other issues so that whether readers are teachers on the professional grade, those with managerial responsibilities within or outside the school, or are involved in helping others design and implement programmes of appraisal and professional development they may be provided with both practical help and further thoughts for reflection.

Christopher Day
Patrick Whitaker
David Wren

Notes on the authors

Christopher Day is Senior Lecturer and Head of the In-Service Unit in the School of Education, University of Nottingham through which he is responsible for an extensive regional programme of professional development activities for teachers. Before moving to his present post he worked in primary and secondary schools, initial teacher training and as a Local Education Authority Adviser. He has worked extensively in in-service teacher education both in the UK and abroad with particular reference to staff and curriculum development and school-based consultancy. As part of his in-service commitments he directs regional and national management courses for heads and staff with management responsibilities in primary schools. His particular interests are in professional learning and changing, and his recent publications include *Classroom based in-service teacher education: the development and evaluation of a client-centred model* (Sussex University, 1981), *Managing Primary Schools: a Professional Development Approach* (Harper and Row, 1985) and *Staff Development in the Secondary School: Management Perspectives* (Croom Helm, 1986).

Patrick Whitaker has been General Adviser for Primary Education in Derbyshire since 1979. Prior to that he held two primary headships in Leicestershire. Among his publications are *The Primary Head* (Heinemann Educational Books, 1983), and with Christopher Day and David Johnstone *Managing Primary Schools: a Professional Development Approach* (Harper and Row, 1985). He has been active as a trainer in the educational management field since 1974 and has helped to develop more active and experiential approaches to in-service education. In recent years his in-service work has increasingly focused on human relations training and applications of counselling theory and practice to the management of schools.

David Wren has spent most of his teaching career involved in staff development activities. He began his primary teaching career in Leicestershire in the early 1960s and was invited to work with the advisory service to help establish and develop a scheme for the induction of probationary teachers in primary schools. In 1968 he moved to Hertfordshire to set up the first Teachers' Centre in Hertford and was actively involved in a wide range of staff development and curriculum development projects for teachers in East Herts. He moved to Derbyshire in 1976 and spent time as a general adviser for primary schools in the urban and suburban schools of Derby as well as the smaller village communities of West Derbyshire and the High Peak district. He now leads the primary advisory team in the authority as the County Adviser for Primary Education.

1 The context of appraisal and professional development

This chapter traces the political, economic and social factors which have affected the growth and tenor of the demands made upon teachers for more public accountability through appraisal. In providing the contexts of appraisal it sets the scene for the succeeding chapters to consider appraisal as a part of every primary school teacher's and headteacher's professional development. Whilst we recognise that central government and local education authorities have a right to lay down legislation and guidelines for schools and teachers we seek to demonstrate that appraisal and professional development models planned in schools and based on principles of ownership, contracting and professional accountability provide the most valuable opportunities for teachers to work together collaboratively and co-operatively to improve and extend their practice and enhance the education of the children they teach.

The last decade has seen the development of a better qualified, better trained and better managed teaching force willing to tackle a whole range of new areas of learning and experience in an effort to offer a better education to children. A wealth of professional literature has poured into staff rooms over the last few years covering topics as diverse as computers and community education, gender issues and geography, sex education and safety on school journeys; and there has been no shortage of advice offered. Yet it would be an understatement to say that primary school teachers feel unhappy, helpless, confused and threatened. So much media coverage seems aimed at undermining the professionalism of teachers and blaming them for the nation's ills that it is difficult to bring a sense of proportion or scale into any discussion on education without appearing to be on the defensive. Why is the education service under the microscope? Why is the climate so much more demanding? Why is morale so low? Why has legislation been introduced to make teachers accountable for their performance in a way never before expected or accepted?

It was at Ruskin College, Oxford, in October, 1976 when the then Labour Prime Minister James Callaghan launched the 'Great Debate' and threw the education establishment into a turmoil which is still affecting our schools. He asserted that the public's interest and concern in education was legitimate in view of the financial investment made in education and that it would be to the advantage of all involved in the educational field if these concerns were aired and shortcomings righted or fears put to rest. Callaghan's notion that education must serve the nation's economic needs and that 'the educational system was out of touch with the fundamental need for Britain to survive economically in a highly competitive world through the efficiency of its industry and commerce' opened the floodgates for some politicians, economists, parents and educators to vent their prejudices, justified or not, upon the education service. For a Prime Minister to bring the issue of education to the forefront of the nation's mind was one thing: for him to ask local education authorities, schools and teachers questions about their practice was another. Were the standards in schools high enough? Were the schools sufficiently accountable to the community? Were they meeting the needs of the nation? Standards, accountability and the curriculum took centre stage and more than a decade later they still remain.

The origins of the Callaghan speech at Ruskin College lay partly in such symbols as William Tyndale Primary School (Auld 1976) and Risinghill Comprehensive School (Berg 1968), partly in complaints from many local authorities about public expenditure cuts and continued critical comment from the Conservative Party and Black Paper writers throughout the 1970s. Tyndale and Risinghill received much media coverage and the links between falling standards, progressive teaching methods and the rest of the nation's ills were quickly made. Both of these events had been important in establishing that there were 'limits to teachers' freedom in deciding on the curriculum' (Lawton 1981). At the same time, however, the political focus on utilitarianism and 'value for money' may be related to broader economic factors and perception – still prevalent – that there is a direct cause and effect link between the quality of education and the economic well-being of the nation. The fact is that throughout the 1970s politicians, local and national, were beginning to take a more active interest in the curriculum, pedagogy and evaluation of schools. The activities at William Tyndale School in Islington merely focused the nation's attention more quickly on the doubts about the education service that already existed in the minds of some politicians and parents. The public enquiry which followed supported a 'back to basics' movement which, despite receiving no official support, still continues.

There has been no shortage of investment by governments in increasing the public visibility of schools and their accountability to the community at large. In 1974 the DES established the 'Assessment of Performance Unit' in order to try to provide criteria through the development of a system for monitoring standards nationally, and the Taylor Report (1977) sought to strengthen the influence of the consumer on the curriculum. One immediate result of the concern over standards was that HMI became involved in two major surveys to see what was actually going on in a large sample of the nation's primary and secondary schools. The findings were eventually published in 1978 (DES 1978) and 1979 (DES 1979). Interestingly, the results from these surveys did not support the contentions of the most critical. Rather they confirmed that the primary schools were spending too much time on the basic skills and needed to offer a broader, richer curriculum diet (DES 1984).

Although there is no centrally imposed direction of the curriculum at the moment, most primary schools follow a similar core of subjects and the learning process is still dominated by the basic cognitive skills (Barker-Lunn 1984, DES 1985). Thus calls for more time and attention to be given to a 'core' curriculum (Baker 1987) would seem to be simply requests to confirm what is already the case. In addition to the pressure upon schools and teachers resulting from these reports, since the 1970s there has been a wealth of written advice made available to LEAs from the DES and from HMI. Schools have had to spend more and more time responding to policy statements and discussion documents which have been floated out on a raft of paper from the authorities themselves and which are all designed to feed the debate and make the service more efficient and more effective. The late Schools Council, individual LEA reports, research publications and writings from educators at universities and colleges have all added to the load.

More recently, the government has shown itself to be much more willing to intervene in the curriculum itself. In 1981 the DES published *The School Curriculum* which represented 'the first explicit and definitive attempt by Central Government for over half a century to steer curricula in a particular direction' (White 1981). This was followed by DES Circular 6/81 which required LEAs to consult with all schools and to provide written statements on curricula where they did not already exist. At about the same time other developments were occurring:

1. The declining birth rate and an accompanying fall in resource provision were affecting curricula and morale of schools.
2. The opportunities for individual teachers to gain promotion either within their own school or by moving to another were diminishing.
3. HMI were making suggestions for changes in the management structures of schools in order to assist in decision-making processes (DES 1977).
4. The Government disbanded the Schools Council, setting in its place two bodies – a Schools Examination Council and a Schools Curriculum Development Committee (the use of 'Council' and 'Committee' possibly indicating the relative importance attached to each body by the Secretary of State).
5. The increasing dissatisfaction with the content of the curriculum by a significant majority of pupils, coupled with the rise in youth unemployment particularly led to increasing external intervention in the curriculum for the 14-18 year olds by agencies such as the Manpower Services Commission through pre-vocational and other schemes of work.
6. The Taylor Report (1977) set the seal on a process which is still occurring in which parents and others are to have increased power to influence the curriculum.
7. The Warnock Report (DES 1978) and the resulting legislation has meant that schools have had to plan a curriculum to fit a broader ability range than previously.
8. The Secretary of State for Education and Science, in a speech at the North of England Education Conference in January 1984, called for a nationally defined curriculum for pupils aged 5-16. This was followed by 'A Note by the Department of Education and Science and Welsh Office' entitled 'The Organisa-

tion and Content of the 5-16 Curriculum'. Essentially, this was a follow up to Circulars 6/81 (above) and 8/83. The purpose of the paper was 'to raise questions and invite comments on them, with a view to establishing as wide a measure of agreement as possible', on (a) the objectives of learning at school, (b) the contribution of each main subject area or element, (c) the content of the 5-16 curriculum as a whole and (d) objectives for attainment at the end of the primary phase and for the secondary (11-16) phase. Since then, there have been more DES and HMI Discussion Papers offering more 'guidelines' for curriculum.

The consequences of these and other factors have been a perceived if not actual deterioration in the conditions of service for teachers. There has been more paperwork, and more meetings both in and out of school have had to be held. People from within and outside education have articulated their opinions, beliefs, wishes, concerning the planning, teaching and assessment of the curriculum, and these have had to be processed, weighed and taken into account. Some have perceived this as an exciting opportunity for a new form of partnership between schools and their local and broader community. Others have been less enthusiastic, and, feeling the pressures of extra workloads and diminishing resources, have begun to withdraw the goodwill upon which much of the quality of school life depends. One year of discontent has stretched into another and resentment has grown as more demands have been made for more work and more accountability.

At a local level, growth in the 1980s of political desire to ensure that school standards are maintained and that curriculum content is focused more finely upon social and economic policy has resulted in an increasing politicisation of some advisory services. 'Advisers' have become 'Inspectors' and while many have retained their brief to promote curriculum development in particular subject areas and phases of education, they now have to spend more time monitoring and inspecting schools (through observation, discussion, interviews and reports to Education Committees). Pressure has been put upon heads of schools to make available job descriptions for each member of staff, and to ensure that regular staff reviews take place and are documented. Legislation has now made it mandatory for each school to provide a school policy document for parents. Added to this, schools are now expected to have professional development policies which are to be reviewed annually.

Arrangements for in-service teacher education (DES Circular 6/86) have also been designed to ensure a more systematic identification of the professional development needs of schools, teachers and LEAs; and these will inevitably be linked to systems of teacher performance appraisal. The arrangements give more control of in-service funding to central government and LEAs and, potentially, fewer opportunities for individually perceived needs of teachers to be met.

Yet the ways in which employers have gone about obtaining value for money, as if there is a direct instrumental measurable outcome of education, improving standards (which by every objective yardstick have in fact risen over the last twenty years), and holding teachers and schools more publicly answerable to them for their curricula and teaching would appear to fly in the face of much of the accumulated knowledge on how teachers learn. It will not be surprising, therefore, if attempts to change schools and teachers continue to be met with some resistance. (See Chapter 2 for a full discussion of this.) The publication of th Government White Paper *Teaching Quality* (DES 1984) added a significant dimension to the 'Great Debate' for this first gave the Government's view that, 'formal assessment of teacher performance is necessary and should be based on classroom visiting by the teacher's head or head of department and an appraisal of both pupils' work and the teacher's contribution to the life of the school'. The walls surrounding the 'secret garden' of the teacher's classroom were about to be breached. The more recent White Paper, *Better Schools*, reaffirmed the Government's view that '... all teachers need help in assessing their own professional performance in building on their strengths and working on the limitations so identified...' (DES 1985). *Quality in Schools: Evaluation and Appraisal* contributed to the inexorable move towards formal and systematic appraisal by 'collecting evidence about the extent and effectiveness of practices for teacher assessment and self-evaluation in schools' (DES 1985) and the Graham Report *Those Having Torches* (The Graham Report 1985) which had been commissioned by the DES, provided a practical framework for planning and operating appraisal schemes.

The LEA's role

It is now accepted generally that regular and formal appraisal of the performance of all teachers is necessary if LEAs are to have the reliable, comprehensive and up-to-date information necessary to facilitate effective professional support and development and to deploy teaching staff to the best advantage. (*Better Schools Summary Document* DES 1985.) The place of the local education authority in any system of appraisal is clear. As the teachers' employer the LEA must introduce, implement and monitor the system across its schools ensuring that criteria are agreed and methods are comparable and consistent. It will need to consider the appraisal of headteachers and other members of the education service. It will need to allow for the variety found within its schools whether they have two teachers or twenty-two teachers and be able to offer continuing guidance and support. It will need to look hard at the resource implications.

The local education authority also will need to help schools and teachers develop a common language. 'Appraisal', 'assessment' and 'evaluation' have become interchangeable and 'self-appraisal' and 'self-evaluation' can refer to the process in which the teacher considers the result of a lesson or topic, or the teacher's performance as seen by others or the work of the school as a whole. The following guidance on terminology is offered in paragraph 9 of *Quality in Schools: Evaluation and Appraisal* (DES 1985):

evaluation is a general term used to describe any activity by the institution or the LEA where the quality of provision is the subject of systematic study;
review indicates a retrospective activity and implies the collection and examination of evidence and information;
appraisal emphasises the forming of qualitative judgements about an activity, a person, or an organisation;

assessment implies the use of measurement and/or grading based on known criteria.

In paragraph 10 a distinction is made between staff development and staff appraisal. Whereas the former, 'is concerned with general matters of in-service needs and career development and may be based on staff appraisal', the latter, 'involves qualitative judgements about performance and, although it may start as self-appraisal by the teacher, it will normally involve judgements by other persons responsible for that teacher's work'. Thus appraisal may well (and usually does) include the identification of professional development needs (DES 1985). We would suggest that this distinction is arbitrary and that the separation of appraisal from staff development serves only the interests of those with a 'top down' view of management.

While some local authorities are further ahead than others in their planning and implementation of schemes, most have many common elements. All are awaiting the final guidance from central government. This itself may be heavily influenced by the results of widely differing appraisal schemes developed in the six 'pilot' LEAs, selected by the Secretary of State, which are piloting projects as a consortium for the Department of Education and Science and funded by an Educational Support Grant of £4 million, spread over three years.

The six schemes raise a range of issues. The Croydon approach includes the principle that teacher appraisal should be related to pupil attainment. Cumbria and Salford share similar principles of teacher self-evaluation aimed at identifying the training needs of individuals and institutions, Cumbria stresses that the appraisal of the individual cannot be separated from the needs of the school. Newcastle upon Tyne is seeking to find a model way of assessing starting points for appraisal in schools. Suffolk emphasises the need for appraisal at all levels with classroom observation an essential element. All of the schemes have the appraisal of headteachers as a cornerstone.

There is a steering group to oversee the consortium comprising the ACAS working party, representatives of the local authorities, the teachers' associations and the Secretary of State. The ACAS recommendations are seeking to raise the quality of the teaching force, improve job satisfaction, identify in-service training needs and enhance career development. The underlying influence in the guidelines to the scheme is that of the Suffolk model and includes: self-evaluation, an appraisal interview, classroom observation, and an appeals procedure.

The Suffolk model (The Graham Report 1985) is worthy of more detailed consideration for it draws together thinking from existing practice in schools in England and abroad, in industry and in commerce, and current research literature. The study team led by the Chief Education Officer, held the view that 'professional appraisal of all those involved in the education service will improve standards and enhance the image of the service'. The work of the Suffolk team, financed by the DES, comes down heavily against linking merit pay to teacher appraisal. They found that teachers were not necessarily antipathetic but had genuine fears and worries about it. Among its conclusions and recommendations are the following:

Purposes

- 'the cornerstone of appraisal schemes is the belief that teachers wish to improve their performance in order to enhance their pupils education';
- appraisal systems should 'develop teachers professionally';
- the 'process' should be characterised by negotiation and agreement about priorities and targets and should be 'constructive, honest, professional and should not threaten the individuality or personality of the teacher';
- schemes operate more effectively where these are 'clear contractual obligations';
- 'teachers' creativity and spontaneity should not be inhibited by the process; on the contrary, idosyncratic effectiveness should be encouraged';
- there should be 'external scrutiny' of the process, and it should be 'capable of convincing and reassuring parents, ratepayers and taxpayers'.

Aims and Objectives: every school scheme should aim to:

- 'improve learning opportunities for all pupils';
- 'improve the management and support of the learning process';
- 'improve the "tone" which influences all work in the school'.

For the teacher the process should:

- 'recognise and support effective practice';
- 'identify areas for development and improvement';
- 'identify and develop potential'.

It suggests that a scheme must enable teachers whose performance falls below par to be identified so that steps can be taken by the school and LEA to rectify the situation, and exceptionally, to terminate employment'.

Elements of appraisal

Classroom observation

Many of the early schemes of appraisal were developed from industry and commerce. Most recent schemes are showing signs of a movement away from the old industrial model, with its hierarchical structure, towards peer appraisal. However, as Nuttall (1986) observes, 'the predominant model is the industrial one centred on target-setting and the evaluation of targets set on previous occasions, coupled with an identification of appropriate career development plans and training needs'. In one respect at least, however, appraisal schemes in the education service differ from those elsewhere. Wilcox (1986) states that 'the observation of performance – particularly if attempted on some kind of systematic basis – would appear to distinguish teacher appraisal from many of the appraisal systems which operate in industry, commerce and the other public services'. Classroom observation features in many of the systems under discussion today. Certainly appraisal would not be popular with many primary school teachers if it was confined to a discussion in a single interview held only annually.

Peer involvement

Appraisal in the form envisaged by a number of school-initiated schemes relies heavily on joint peer negotiation and evaluation and much good work can develop from this. Familiarity with the primary school classroom, its children and its curriculum is an advantage provided that criteria for observation are agreed and based on good educational and professional grounds. 'Good' may, of course, have different definitions according to context, purposes and value systems held by particular governments, LEAs, teachers, schools and parents! The notion of the 'critical friend' or trusted colleague is a valuable one and should be encouraged, but it must be professionally managed so that it is more than a cosy chat between colleagues.

Peer appraisal may offer an answer to the difficult question, 'Who appraises the headteacher?' The hierarchical or line-management approach, if adopted by the LEA, could present serious logistical problems with so many primary headteachers and so few primary advisers or inspectors. A group of experienced heads, working as a team, or as individuals could assist in the process. A number of other ideas have been discussed, including panels or teams comprising education officers, advisers and experienced heads; a teacher or teachers from within the school; or a combination of these groups. LEAs will have to find an answer to this question quickly, and a similar question about the appraisal of officers, inspectors and advisers, for the Authority scheme could lack credibility if it was seen not to apply to all of its employees.

Community involvement

Teachers, headteachers, parents, governors, LEAs and central government all have significant parts to play in appraisal. The school governing body and the parent body may have a special part to play in the process too. Governors who will be drawn from the parent body and will include representatives from the community as 'consumers' will have an increasingly important role within the school. They could offer a more distanced, dispassionate view to add to the more subjective, involved views of the clients.

Support

If the word 'appraisal' raises concerns in the mind of the teacher so the design of an effective system will be a concern of those who seek to introduce it. By allowing a free and frank exchange of ideas in an interview, by offering advice and support after a period of classroom observation, by introducing a staff development policy in the school expectations will be raised. Ideas offered as support and advice may be interpreted as promises of action, statements about developing particular aspects of work may be construed as time out for course work. If no clear use is made of the outcomes of appraisal then teachers will quickly become frustrated and cynical. The resource implications could be such that the school or the LEA would find it impossible to move forward after the first attempt. Good sense must prevail, promises which cannot be fulfilled must not be made. Yet a major concern has been the increasing pressure on time and resources for appraisal. The Suffolk scheme suggests three days as the minimum amount of time for training appraisers, and that between eight and twelve hours per teacher are needed for in-school appraisal each year. Additional costs are implied for the in-service consequences of appraisal and increased administration. And who will be teaching the children while all this is going on? Already there are signs in many authorities that the supply teaching pool is drying up.

Legislation

It is no longer a question of if appraisal arrives, but when. In reality it is with us now. The Education Bill 1986, confirmed by the Education (No 2) Act 1986 'enables' local education authorities to implement appraisal in schools. Before any regulations are made there will be wide consultation. Consultation is not something many teachers or schools feel they have experienced in the past and the current dispute over pay and conditions of service has left many teachers feeling helpless and increasingly concerned about a number of issues over which they feel they have little control. The unprecedented intervention in the life of schools by those outside has demoralised many of those working inside the schools.

Section 49 of Chapter 61 of this Act is headed 'Appraisal of performance of teachers' and is worth quoting at length (though we should be mindful of Circular 8/86 which states that this section is only a regulation-making power).

49 (1) The Secretary of State may by regulations make provision requiring local education authorities, or such other persons as may be prescribed, to secure that the performance of teachers to whom the regulations apply
 (a) in discharging their duties; and
 (b) in engaging in other activities connected with the establishments at which they are employed;
 is regularly appraised in accordance with such requirements as may be prescribed.
 (2) The regulations may, in particular, make provision
 (a) requiring the governing bodies of such categories of schools or other establishments as may be prescribed
  (i) to secure, so far as it is reasonably practicable for them to do so, that any arrangements made in accordance with the regulations are compiled with in relation to their establishments; and
  (ii) to provide such assistance to the local education authority as the authority may reasonably require in connection with their obligations under the regulations;
 (b) with respect to the disclosure to teachers of the results of appraisals and the provision of opportunities for them to make representations with respect to those results; and
 (c) requiring local education authorities to have regard to the results of appraisals in the exercise of such of their functions as may be prescribed.

(3) Before making any regulations under subsection (1) above, the Secretary of State shall consult
   (a) such associations of local authorities and representatives of teachers, as appear to him to be concerned; and
   (b) any other person with whom consultation appears to him to be desirable.

Recent actions by the Secretary of State have reinforced the view that at the heart of the problem lies the deep-seated constitutional difficulty over the relationship between central and local government. Issues such as teachers' pay and conditions of service, a national curriculum with 'bench marks', the enhanced position of governing bodies, together with appraisal of teacher performance combine to threaten both teacher and local education authority autonomy.

In the area of pay and conditions of service alone, central government has made such rapid strides that the Burnham Committee has disappeared and been replaced by the Teachers' Pay and Conditions Bill. After months of protracted negotiation, with talks in Coventry, Nottingham and London, it seemed that agreement was about to be reached within the more progressive and flexible framework provided by ACAS and by the LEAs and the teacher unions together when the Secretary of State intervened and introduced his own detailed structure. Inevitably, teacher action followed but the pay package linked with new conditions of service now stands and the new Act has removed teachers' negotiating rights at least until 1990. The spectre of 'payment by results' looms and far from encouraging teachers to work even harder to raise educational standards the actions of the Secretary of State have left the teachers confused, demoralised and feeling under-valued by politicians and society in general.

Those seeking to impose appraisal schemes might consider that appraisal is not new to the teaching profession. As part of their daily work teachers appraise their children and in return, the children appraise the teachers (see Chapters 4 and 5). 'That's a nice piece of work, John', 'I think you could do much better, Ann', are comments equally applicable to teachers and to children. Notions of the 'best' child in the class or 'best' teacher in the school are commonplace. It is very evident that new entrants to the profession are appraised during and at the end of the probationary year, that teachers with managerial responsibilities appraise their colleagues, and that teachers seeking promotion are the subject of written references and telephone enquiries. However, the criteria upon which these judgements are made and the extent to which they are objective and systematic are not always clear. One thing we can be certain about is that teachers are not always sure how and when appraisal takes place, nor can they always see the necessity or use for it. With so many different interpretations of 'work' in schools and no common professional language among teachers it is inevitable that suspicion and fear together with genuine concern about 'who will be appraising me' abound.

Appraisal, then, has been launched at a time when morale in the education service is at a low level. Media coverage emphasised aspects relating to the weeding out of incompetent teachers and dismissal. The approaches mentioned seemed to be 'top down' models and the notion of those in the authority collecting evidence and information about schools and classrooms is seen by teachers to be very threatening to their professionalism. It has been natural, then, for schools and teachers to build up lists of reasons why the time is not right to introduce appraisal – and lack of time, and the appropriate resources to enable the process to begin, together with resistance by the teachers' professional associations to the introduction of legislation (HMSO 1986) have enabled the formal introduction of a national scheme to be delayed.

The school context

There is another danger. Staff relationships could suffer badly if the climate is not right and the system not carefully planned. The best appraisal systems are those which are developed locally, where heads and teachers work together to build a system that suits them best, so that they are grounded in the school policy for staff development. Appraisal needs to be conducted within a context of trust and openness and supported by a considered policy for individual and school development which has been agreed by all of those taking part. Only then will confidence and a common sense of purpose have been created. In fact there are already a number of LEA and school initiated schemes in operation (see Chapter 4 for examples of these). Indeed, the development of appraisal has not been confined to government initiatives. In 1976 Surrey was suggesting the idea to its heads when they attended management training courses and HMI identified a number of local authority schemes (DES 1985). Individual schools have been actively developing their own systems of school and teacher review (Turner and Clift 1985). Industrial action has slowed or prevented the development of many of these schemes and the impact of impending local authority and national initiatives has, no doubt, further reduced both the number and pace of developments.

Where school initiated appraisal systems exist they are welcomed by almost everyone. Teachers need feedback and a good appraisal system offers the opportunity to them to know how they are doing – the bits they are doing well, the bits that need development and the bits where problems exist. It also allows time to plan for the future, to discuss the goals for the school and the teacher. But appraisal is not a substitute for effective day to day management of teachers. On its own an annual appraisal interview is a poor way to develop staff. A well thought out school policy of staff development embracing appraisal will be seen as encouraging an awareness of the individual's personal and professional role within the school. (See Chapters 3 and 7 for detailed consideration of the organisational climate and personal and professional relationships.)

The key principle on which this book is built is that appraisal needs to be conducted within a context of trust and openness and supported by a considered policy for individual and school development which has been agreed by all of those taking part. Only then will confidence and a common sense of purpose have been created. It must be seen as an integral part of staff development and should be a process which is devised through the involvement of all of those directly concerned. It must take account of individual circumstances and give the teacher control and ownership of the process and the outcomes must be treated in confidence by those concerned. The consultative aspects of the process are vital to the success of any scheme and the current fears of a national or a local one being imposed are somewhat eased by that statement being reinforced in the new Education (No 2) Act – Section 49 (4) 'Before making any regulations... the Secretary of State shall consult...'

LEAs and schools that are already engaged in appraisal work, and these numbers are increasing rapidly, seem to find their success depends very much on a situation where the climate of the school as a whole encourages and accustoms staff to look critically at their practices and where good communication is seen as an essential ingredient towards establishing a common sense of purpose; where agreed criteria are explicit and where the process is linked to staff development, curriculum development and in-service training. Collaboration and co-operation are commonplace These schools see that appraisal will assist in the identification and fulfilment of potential; that appraisal schemes will provide opportunity to review each teacher's needs, both as an individual and as a member of a team, and that they will support effective practice and give increased job satisfaction. It follows that appraisal must involve all the staff. It should be structured and undertaken regularly focusing on both the learning and the teaching processes. It should focus too, on the job rather than on the individual, and must take account of the contexts in which the staff work. It must provide a vehicle for open, frank and immediate feedback and will need to be capable of change and improvement in the light of experience. Questions relating to confidentiality and ownership will need to be addressed at an early stage as will the notion of an appeals procedure. It cannot be assumed that all teachers will find the appraisal process agreeable but a teacher who disagrees with the appraisor should not feel that there is no procedure for a second opinion.

All of these points have been voiced by the teachers' professional associations for many years and it is very apparent that schemes currently in action or under discussion in schools or LEAs have relied heavily on suggestions made in discussion papers from the main teachers' unions. School-focused staff development, career development, self-appraisal, the appraisal of heads and peer appraisal and opportunity for improvement of performance as a continuous process are recurrent themes.

It has become painfully clear that the government will only listen to the teachers' voice on appraisal if it can be assured that standards will improve, that professional development will take place and that public accountability will be implicit. We accept that appraisal will be required by central government and by the local education authorities, and that a system will be implemented. If, however, we want a scheme which will satisfy teachers' professional needs, meet their goals and benefit both children and community then we must involve ourselves in the making of it. If we are to do this, then we must take into account what are the most effective conditions for teacher and school learning and change; what tools we have at our disposal; and what personal, interpersonal and organisational skills we need in embarking upon the development of a school policy for appraisal and staff development. We hope that the succeeding chapters will help in this process.

2 Teacher learning and change

If appraisal is to have any long-term impact upon teachers and schools then those involved in its design, management and resourcing need to ensure that it is valued by teachers as making a positive contribution to the quality of teaching and learning in their classrooms. In order to achieve this, serious consideration needs to be given - and be seen to be given - to its purposes; to how teachers learn and why they change (or resist changing); and to what should be the most appropriate and productive relationship between employers and teachers; heads and teachers; and teachers and teachers in the design and implementation of appraisal schemes. This chapter focuses upon these issues, and in doing so suggests that appraisal must be centred upon professional development if it is to achieve success. The first part of the chapter places the debate about the purposes and practices of appraisal in the context of accountability. The second part considers appraisal and teacher change. Here we propose certain conditions and principles which are necessary for effective professional learning and outline some of the constraints upon teacher learning which may cause resistance to change. Finally we consider the kinds of leadership interventions which might best promote professional development.

Purposes, principles and outcomes of appraisal

In Chapter 1 we emphasised that appraisal schemes should aim to:
- (a) improve learning opportunities for all pupils;
- (b) improve the management and support of the learning process;
- (c) improve the 'tone', or hidden curriculum, which influences all work in the school.

As far as the teacher is concerned, the process should:
- (a) recognise and support effective practice;
- (b) identify areas of development and improvement;
- (c) identify and develop potential.

(The Graham Report 1985)

These aims seem reasonable enough and imply clearly that the general purpose is the enhancing and enriching of the curriculum for pupils through the improved practice of teachers. Indeed, the Report continues by emphasising that teachers should be supported in their efforts to increase effectiveness, that the process should enhance the quality of pupil learning and that some consideration of teacher career aspiration should be part of the process.

The 'theory' is acceptable. No teacher or school is perfect. It can be assumed that teachers and schools will want to find out how to be more effective and may need support in both the process and the achievement of improved practice. However, it could be argued that most teachers and schools are involved in appraisal already in many ways, ranging from the informal to the formal. Most teachers do reflect upon practice (if only to survive in the classroom!); most schools do hold regular staff discussions on curriculum, classroom organisation and pupil assessment; and most teachers are monitored by their heads and LEAs through headteacher discussion, the provision of forecasts, pupil records, and classroom monitoring. Why, then, is there controversy? We believe that the answer may lie in definitions of accountability. The East Sussex Accountability Project (1979) identified three kinds of accountability:

1 *Answerability* to one's clients, i.e. pupils and parents (moral accountability).
2 *Responsibility* to oneself and one's colleagues (professional responsibility).
3 *Accountability* in the strict sense to one's employers or political masters (contractual accountability).

Although the three overlap, in recent years the emphasis has moved from 'responsibility' to 'answerability' and 'accountability'. The consensus which once allowed schools to operate with relative autonomy has broken down. Now not only are teachers accountable to themselves and their pupils and parents for the education which they provide, but politicians, responsible ultimately for public expenditure in a declining economy in which unemployment is rising, want to see 'value for money'. Where this is seen by teachers as the key justificatory concept for the introduction of formal appraisal schemes, it is not surprising that they are suspicious. After all:

> ... what does a teacher have to gain from having his work examined? As he sees it, absolutely nothing. He is exposing himself to administrators and parents. He risks damage to his ego by finding out he is not doing his job as well as he thinks he is. Perhaps the worst of all he risks discovering that his students do not really care for him, something a teacher would rather not know. The culture of the school offers no rewards for examining one's behaviour – only penalties. Since there are no punishments for not exposing one's behaviour and many dangers in so doing, the prudent teacher gives lip service to the idea and drags both feet...
> (House 1972)

There are three facts which must be emphasised in any discussion of appraisal, since they have a significant bearing on its potential effect and effectiveness. First, teachers did not ask for it; second, whatever scheme is imposed or negotiated between the LEA and schools, it will undoubtedly involve more work on the part of an already overburdened teaching profession for little professional or other reward. Third, regardless of the rhetoric in which the debate on teacher appraisal is wrapped, it is clearly Government inspired, the need having been caused, because, 'a significant number of teachers are performing at a standard below that required to achieve the objectives now proposed for schools' (DES 1985). One cannot, of course, attribute these motives to all those who are engaged in policy making. Professional associations, for example, see appraisal as being an essential part of enhanced professional development opportunities for teachers; and some LEAs would subscribe to this – though as employers it is difficult to see how they can avoid the temptation to use appraisal as a means of control.

We have seen in Chapter 1 that the current discussion on the importance of appraisal as a means of identifying teachers' professional development needs, and as a collaborative endeavour between LEA and school, headteacher and teacher, Government and LEA, is framed by legislation. Regular and formal appraisal of the performance of all teachers is, 'necessary if local education authorities are to have reliable comprehensive and up-to-date information necessary to facilitate effective professional support' (DES 1985). What is really at issue here is a sea of change in the control of teaching. This apparently rational, almost benign statement, cloaks an unprecedented and potentially massive intervention by those from outside the school and classroom upon the lives of those inside. In effect, responsibility and accountability for professional development is now regarded not only as a matter for individual teachers and schools, but as a management duty of every LEA.

The Government's proposals for appraisal have been described as:

> a powerful attack on the limited professionalism that teachers have so far achieved... (They)... push the teacher closer than ever before to become an educational worker who has no control over the content of his work and has to accept the judgement made by his managers.
>
> (Hartley and Broadfoot 1985)

Yet appraisal, if it is to succeed, must be seen as a collaborative process in which both individuals, institutions and LEAs actively accept that, 'It is not simply the actions of individuals which need to be changed to bring about improvements in teaching but also those underlying structures which limit and restrict the options available' (Elliott 1982). It is incumbent on all who are engaged in initiating and forming appraisal policy to ensure that power structures, relationships between LEAs and school, and conditions in schools encourage rather than inhibit teacher learning and this will be more likely to occur where there is full and active participation at all levels. Hierarchical appraisal schemes devised and implemented by those from 'above' as distinct from those which involve participation at all stages are unlikely to have any lasting impact on the quality of teaching and learning in schools and classrooms.

The Graham Report recognises the problem of hierarchical or 'top down' models of appraisal by stating that, 'There is some evidence to show that staff appraisal can degenerate into a paper exercise in which worthless reports are compiled and filed simply to comply with procedural instructions...'

It goes on to emphasise that:

formal appraisal is seen to be only one stage in a continuous process;
teachers understand the purposes of the appraisal process;
classroom observation is seen to be central to the process;
the appraisal interview is conducted in optimum physical conditions and stresses performance rather than personality;
the results of the interview are practical, attainable and support to achieve them is forthcoming;
time and encouragement are given for the attainment of targets;
regular monitoring, moderation and evaluation takes place.'

(The Graham Report 1985)

This positive view of appraisal may go some way towards reconciling the needs of management and the needs of teachers, for: 'the role that the subordinate has played in identifying these (strengths and weaknesses) increases his or her willingness to implement action steps arising out of them' (Fletcher 1984). It will be clear, then, that there is a direct link between appraisal and accountability and that the degree of success or failure achieved by any appraisal scheme will depend upon the way in which its purposes are defined and understood by all those with a stake in the appraisal enterprise and the extent to which these are embedded in the processes and procedures of the schemes.

It could be argued for example that if appraisal is to be useful it must contain systematic collection and examination of evidence and information concerning the quality of educational provision as well as involve teachers in self-monitoring, 'the ongoing, largely informal, process by which those responsible satisfy themselves that teaching is of an acceptable quality' (Eraut 1986). Furthermore, if appraisal is to involve the identification of professional development needs by those responsible for teachers' work, then it would seem appropriate that appraisal of the extent to which these needs have been supported must also occur. Indeed, the assertion in this chapter that appraisal is a two-way process in which both appraisors and appraisees are held to account for the way in which they carry out or 'deliver' their responsibilities is an attempt to reinstate appraisal as a means of 'contributing to the continuing development of teacher autonomy' (Day, Johston and Whitaker 1985).

The rhetoric regarding the outcomes of appraisal is clearly on the side of staff development. For example, the DES (1985) listed them as being:

- modified behaviour/approaches by the teacher;
- presentation of opportunities/experience for further and better informed staff development;
- training opportunities (on and off site);
- changes of job to widen or deepen experience and give a better teacher-task match.

The problem of the 'new' appraisal schemes may be encapsulated by linking the purposes of appraisal with its outcomes:

... it is the product which will decide the real purpose of appraisal. If the product is an action plan for development, then the appraisal interview will become a staff development interview with another name... But if the product is an agreed appraisal of a teacher's performance for insertion into their file, the appraisal foreground will put staff development purposes very much into the background...

(Eraut 1986)

Here the immense possibilities and problems of an appraisal system are revealed. Where it is centred on the needs of management and conceived as primarily a 'contribution to the positive and efficient management and deployment of the teaching force' (The Graham Report 1985), rather than a means of supporting and enhancing the quality of teaching and learning in schools it is unlikely to meet with unqualified success.

A reconciliation between the interests of teachers and employers is provided by the scheme in which HAY Management Consultants (1986) promote the concept of 'performance management' rather than 'appraisal', the latter being seen as having threatening undertones. They place self-evaluation at the heart of the concept. Performance management is defined as:

> the conscious determination of a teacher's responsibilities (accountabilities) which we used to determine objectives (goals) and identify needs and contraints which could prevent the attainment of those goals. It is an aid to self-evaluation by the teacher

The advantage of this kind of approach is it can be tailored to the needs of individual schools and teachers who would, therefore, have a sense of ownership. The claim is that:

1 it is a benefit to individuals in a 'people business';
2 it offers fair and rational feedback;
3 it links what has been learned to planned development;
4 it is a corporate effort school-wide;
5 it begins with self-appraisal.

If, in the final analysis, appraisal schemes are to be judged by the contribution which they make to the quality of teaching and learning in the classroom (and the question as to how those responsible for implementing policies and systems of appraisal intend to evaluate them has yet to be addressed) then self-appraisal must be a central and continuing element; and this is considered in detail in Chapters 4 and 5. However, there are a number of other conditions which must be met. Appraisal policies and systems must, in the first instance, be accepted by teachers as being worthwhile, relevant and practical in order to secure their willing participation. They must:

1 be designed and implemented by means of an acceptable blend of centralized and delegated control;
2 be fair and perceived as fair by all the parties involved;
3 be capable of identifying strengths as well as suggesting appropriate practical remedies to problems identified;
4 be embedded in each school's staff and curriculum development policy;
5 be economic in their use of resources (including teacher time and energy);

6 yield accounts which are intelligible to and believed by their intended audiences (credible and valid);
7 begin and end with self-appraisal.

Yet even where LEAs encourage schools and teachers to participate in the design and implementation of appraisal schemes there is bound to be, at the very least, a residue of suspicion and scepticism as to the real purposes of the exercise. We believe that if appraisal is to have any significant effect upon teachers' thinking and practice, those involved in the design and implementation of appraisal schemes must take into consideration how teachers learn and provide both the conditions and leadership appropriate to supporting this learning and the changes which may result.

Teacher learning and change

The assumption throughout this chapter, and indeed the book, is that professional development cannot be forced. Teachers cannot be developed (passively), but can best develop (actively). Teachers gain new perspectives, increase their knowledge and skills as a natural part of their working lives. The problem is that although much teacher learning occurs naturally, gradually and by a variety of means, for years teaching has been an activity in which work has been planned, carried out and assessed for the most part privately. So much of this growth is unnoticed (by those outside the school), many changes are slow and unperceived (often even by the teacher); and the growth in learning is not linear. It follows, then, that:

1 teachers' learning is bound to be limited if it always occurs in the isolation of their own classrooms;
2 there is a need for intervention by trusted others who may help teachers check upon their perceptions, for example, the match between their intentions (what they want to achieve) and their practices (how they behave);
3 appraisal linked directly to professional development is one means of helping teachers to increase their effectiveness;
4 successful appraisal will take several factors into account, i.e. the knowledge and experience of the teacher, the school context, professional contact and discussion outside the school, and the extent to which teachers themselves identify the need, can foresee practical benefits for themselves and their pupils, and are given the time, resources (and where necessary skills) which will enable them to take an active role in the design, implementation and evaluation of the process.

However carefully articulated and realistic programmes of appraisal are, they must take into account the human factor. This is necessary first because development of any kind inevitably involves people in a reappraisal of values, attitudes and feelings as well as practice, and these are, by definition, not governed by rationality nor amenable to prescription; and second, because attempts to promote appraisal as part of staff development are unlikely to meet with success unless there is an active consideration of the psychological and social dynamic in its planning, process and evaluation.

...effective change depends on the genuine commitment of those required to implement it, and that commitment can only be achieved if those involved feel that they have control of the process.... Teachers will readily seek to improve their practice if they regard it as part of their professional accountability, whereas they are likely to resist change that is forced on them

(MacCormick and James 1983)

Essentially it must be recognised that the process of appraisal will involve a shift in perceptions, roles and activities. It will mean that private assumptions and practices must be shared with and opened up for questioning by others. Those involved will be asked to question aspects of their thinking, attitudes and practices and present some or all of these for the scrutiny of others. Thus the process of appraisal is unlikely to be comfortable – even where extensive negotiations have taken place, contracts have been made and forms of confidentiality ensured. Consciously suspending judgement about one's own work will almost inevitably 'raise doubts about what under ordinary circumstances appears to be effective or wise practice' (Sergiovanni 1984). Yet the raising of doubts is only the first in what will be a number of potentially painful steps along the road to change – a road which can be littered with obstacles of time, energy, resources and, perhaps most important, self-doubt.

If we begin from the premise that '...the ultimate arbiter of whether some finding has implications for practice is the person engaged in practice...' (Fenstermacher 1983) then it follows that teachers have the capacity to be self-critical. Many (hopefully most) teachers will be 'connoisseurs' or potential connoisseurs who are able not only to distinguish between what is significant about one set of teaching and learning practices and another, to recognise and appreciate different facets of their teaching and colleagues' or pupils' learning, but also, as critics, to 'disclose the qualities of events or objects that connoisseurship perceives' (Eisner 1979). Appraisal schemes should recognise and capitalise upon teachers' capacity to be self-critical. They should assume a store of practical knowledge about practice and have built in opportunities for this to be made explicit, where appropriate, and utilised. One way of doing this is through the support and development of self-monitoring strategies. (These are discussed fully in Chapter 4 and 5). Yet the capacities to be self-critical and develop self-monitoring strategies are often limited by socialisation, psychological and practical factors such as time, energy and isolation, and it is worth spending a little time considering these.

Many of the actions that teachers take in their classrooms are based on implicit expectations, attitudes and values. They:

> ...are acutely aware of some of these expectations, particularly those emphasised in transactions with people outside the school, but less aware of others. Some professional norms are so internalised that they only become apparent when somebody questions them or some unusual incident draws attention to them...
> (Eraut, Barton and Canning 1978)

Our explicit actions both as educationists and practitioners, are therefore often based on our implicit, unstated knowledge of the nature of practice in any given setting (Polyani 1967). Current practices are, in a sense, rules of action which allow us both to maintain a stable view of, for example, the classroom or the school, and give priority to certain kinds of information while ignoring other kinds. They are theories of control. New teachers very quickly develop assumptions about practices which allow them to cope with the complexities of teaching and being members of staff. They develop what Yinger (1979) has labelled as 'routines'. Once a personal solution has been reached, and we have found 'what works for us', then our routines and decision habits serve to keep mental effort at a reasonable level. Since it is rare for these to be made explicit or tested, the possibilities for evaluating those values, expectations and assumptions which underpin teaching are minimal. This evolution and internalisation of a theory of action is one aspect of learning to become a teacher and coping in the classroom.

Argyris and Schon (1976) characterise this normal world of learning as 'single loop'. While single-loop learning is necessary as a means of maintaining continuity in the highly predictable activities that make up the bulk of our lives, it also limits the possibilities of change. It is argued that if we allow our theory of action to remain unexamined indefinitely, our minds will thus be closed to much valid information and the possibilities for change will be minimal. In effect, if we only maintain our field of constancy we become 'prisoners of our programs' and only see what we want to see. Our rule of thumb decisions, once discovered, are rarely submitted to critical analysis, even though they may no longer be appropriate. This is an argument for engaging from time to time in what Argyris and Schon (1976) call 'double-loop' learning. This involves allowing things which have previously been taken for granted to be seen as problematic, and opening oneself to new perspectives and new sources of evidence. Essentially, one has to be prepared to see oneself as others see one in order to better understand one's behavioural world, and one's effect upon it (Eraut 1977).

What, then, are the best conditions for teacher learning and professional development? Clearly, the responsibility of the 'managers' must be to minimise constraints upon learning itself and indeed upon the motivation to learn. By implication, they must not impose, but negotiate, they must work with schools and teachers in identifying needs, they must accept that learning and change is a lengthy, time consuming business and, in doing so, they must recognise and resource the need for teacher reflection, evaluation and planning within the school day with appropriate human and financial support. The grant related in-service training scheme (DES 6/86 Local Education Authority Training Grants Scheme) enables LEAs to begin to provide more resources, for example, in terms of supply cover for teachers in support of school-focused work, and the use of pupil-teacher staffing ratios to create the possibility of teachers being in school but not necessarily always in face-to-face contact with pupils. (Paradoxically, the legislation described in Chapter 1 may well act against this.) However, the scheme re-emphasises the LEAs' responsibilities for the quality of in-service provision. One consequence of this is that they must adopt interventionist roles which are seen to take account of the accumulated knowledge on teacher learning and change.

Another is that they must take account of teachers' learning needs; and this next section of the chapter will focus upon five principles for maximising the conditions for effective professional learning in the context of appraisal.

1 Learning requires opportunities for reflection and self-confrontation.
2 Teachers and schools are motivated to learn by the identification of an issue or problem which concerns them.
3 Teachers learn best through active experiencing/participation.
4 Decisions about change should arise from reflections upon and confrontation of past and present practice.
5 Schools and teachers need support throughout processes of change.

Internal constraints and the need for reflection and self-confrontation

> The best way to improve practice lies not so much in trying to control people's behaviour as in helping them control their own by becoming more aware of what they are doing
>
> (Elliott 1977)

In his survey of research in this area, Smyth (1984) reports that adults learn when they are provided with opportunities for continuous guided reflection, based on 'lived experience'. He suggests that adults (and teachers) learn by doing and benefit most from those situations which combine action and reflection. Elliott (1984) comments upon the 'lack of a rich stock of self-generated professional knowledge', seeing the cause of this as being the traditional isolation of teachers' practice; while the ILEA Report (1984) notes that 'a well intentioned respect for professional autonomy can lead some teachers to become prisoners within their classrooms'. *Clearly, then, the message would seem to be that appraisal and professional development should present opportunities for less teacher isolation and more time for reflection upon action, outside as well as inside the classroom.*

Most, if not all teachers, often engage in what Schon describes as 'reflection-in-action... a reflective conversation with the situation' (Schon 1983). Indeed, this is a significant means of generating new knowledge (e.g. of children's learning processes), skills (e.g. in responding to children) and concepts (e.g. of the communication of knowledge). In fact, 'reflection-in-action' is a necessary part of survival in the classroom for, at least initially, it serves to reduce many variables which exist in any given situation, thus empowering teachers 'to re-make and if necessary re-order the world in which they live' (Smyth 1987).

Teachers and schools are motivated to learn by the identification of an issue or problem which concerns them (i.e. which they own)

If it is recognized that teachers are active learners then it follows that an issue or problem which others identify may be perceived as irrelevant or not worthwhile unless they themselves can be convinced of its validity. Furthermore, most teachers share needs of:

- Affiliation: the need for a sense of belonging (to a team)
- Achievement: the need for a sense of 'getting somewhere' in what is done
- Appreciation: the need for a sense of being appreciated for the efforts one makes
- Influence: the need for a sense of having some influence over what happens

within the work setting;
- Ownership: the need for a sense of personal investment in the process of appraisal and its outcomes.

Teachers learn best through active experiencing/participating

To be self-critical is to be able to participate in one's own learning. There is much accumulated evidence to suggest that teachers learn best when they are actively involved in determining the focus of their learning. Participation for teachers, as for children, provides opportunities, 'for the development of decision-making skills, enlarges their perspectives and helps them become better informed about their own roles, responsibilities and problems of their colleagues' (Simons 1982). Although writing in the context of whole school evaluation, the claims for participation which the author outlines would apply equally to appraisal. There is no assumption that all teachers wish to be self-directing. Some, like children, may wish to be 'told' things, or may have an expectation that they should be told. Indeed, where teachers are participants in their own learning and appraisal, problems may arise because their inquiry skills are under or undeveloped. Indeed for some teachers who, for example, may be 'currently encountering conditions of decisional equilibrium or saturation, increasing participation may actually prove to be highly dysfunctional' (Aluth and Belasco 1972).

Although there is research which indicates that not all teachers wish to participate or indeed derive satisfaction from doing so (Duke, Showers, and Imber, 1980), this is more often than not the product of role expectation, personality factors or socialisation. There are schools and LEAs in which teachers have long been treated as 'passive consumers within their own organizational structure' (House 1974) and where 'time constraints and the control ethos of bureaucracy stand in the way of a teacher forging regular contacts with a range of different educators. This is not a situation which lends itself to obtaining and reflecting upon new ideas (Morrison, Osborne and McDonald 1977). The clear message here is that appraisal systems which do not fully involve teachers at all stages are, in effect, acting against their best learning interests.

Decisions about change should arise from reflections upon and confrontation of past and present practice

If teachers are expected to take part in the seven distinct sequential phases of appraisal suggested in the Graham Report (1985):

- Preparation   gathering information; agreeing priority areas; looking at job descriptions
- Classroom information   'the most practical procedure for collecting information about teacher performance'
- Interview   a 'genuine dialogue'; need for time and privacy; a performance assessment leading to the identification of future targets

- Results   the agreement of practical and realistic targets
- Monitoring   Follow up process not only checking achievement but providing support as teacher attempts to meet targets
- Moderation   LEA's responsibility to ensure uniformity
- Evaluation   to be carried out by 'a local review body comprised of professional personnel'

then time and assistance are required.

Confrontation of one's practice may, for example, involve a temporary 'deskilling' (MacDonald 1973); and elsewhere in this book we discuss the kinds of support which may be made available. Certainly, though, teachers who are involved in appraisal as part of a professional development process must be offered appropriate affective and intellectual support, be assisted in the collection and generation of information from the classroom and assisted in the validation of this.

Schools and teachers need support throughout processes of change

If teacher learning (as a result of appraisal) is indeed a long-term process of up to two years duration involving experimentation, reflection and problem solving (Eraut 1983) then appraisal systems which do not invest in this long term support will not, in effect, be able to support the professional development of schools and teachers. This will create a credibility problem for those who manage.

Resistance to change

The problem with moving towards the kind of 'double-loop' learning suggested by teacher appraisal is that attention is drawn to myriads of additional variables of information which are normally 'filtered out' by teachers. They may no longer respond only intuitively to situations, but are forced, through confrontation with self, into a critical and rational response. Stenhouse (1975) called this, 'disciplined intuition' rather than 'rationalist abstraction' and perceived the need for external support for change which must grow from within the individual. Other problems include the burden of incompetence, practicality ethic, fear of disclosure, time and energy, and a lack of self-confidence.

The burden of incompetence

MacDonald and Rudduck (1971) have pointed out that if teachers take the risk of departing from their niche in the social and organisational structures of the school into which they have been socialised in order to innovate, they risk taking on 'the burden of incompetence' where the approved certainties they have striven to construct since their own days as beginning teachers are laid to one side and they once again become vulnerable to socialisation pressure to return to the norm, much as when they first began.

The practicality ethic

Elliott (1977) elaborates the point in discussing Doyle and Ponder's account of the 'practicality ethic in teacher decision-making'. The argument runs that when teachers talk about change proposals:

> ... we will find that the term 'practical' is frequently and consistently used to label them and this labelling represents an evaluative process which is the central ingredient in the initial decision teachers make regarding the implementation of a proposed change in classroom procedure.

We can detect here the familiar forces of socialisation. If change is not 'practical' in terms of providing for the individuals their necessary peer support, their group references, their standing subject specialists, their prestige as respected practitioners of what their school wishes to practice and values, then it will indeed face rejection.

It seems clear then, that for the individual, once in the system all the incentives lie in one direction – to stay a functional part of the system: socialisation forces hold the structure in a steady state.

Disclosure

Change is difficult because it involves disclosure, and disclosure can be threatening to self-confidence and self-esteem. It is not surprising, therefore, that teachers have developed sophisticated systems for resisting external attempts to intervene in their classrooms, the most significant contexts of their working lives, the heart of the professional practice.

Few people will readily abandon a relatively stable constant world over which they have at least some control – be it in the classroom or through established curricular, assessment procedures, academic and pastoral core structures, or communication patterns – unless they can see advantages for themselves, their staffs and their pupils. If they cannot, then they may use a repertoire of devices in order to protect themselves. They may:

- adopt the language of change, but retain old behaviour;
- become selectively inattentive to information that points to problems (i.e. ignore it);
- change jobs or change roles within the same institution;
- make marginal changes to behaviour;
- use authority to elicit the desired behaviour from others, so that they conform to desired change.

Time and energy

Few teachers have the time or energy to reflect systematically on their thinking and practice. Most engage in what Elliott (1983), writing in the context of self-evaluation and professional development, calls, 'unreflective self-evaluation based on tacit practical knowledge'. (He defines practical knowledge as that which 'is derived from their own and others' past experience' (Elliott 1983).) Elliott goes on to argue that for teachers to be truly autonomous, responsible and answerable they must have opportunities to engage in 'deliberative inquiry' on past, current and future practice. (See also Reid 1978.) Thus there is a recognition that the quality of the teacher's reflective framework is a decisive factor in his or her development and that opportunities for the growth of clarity and awareness of one's own thinking and behaviour must therefore be built in as essential items in any appraisal system.

Communication

A related problem which arises from the tradition of private testing and learning in the teaching profession is the inability of many teachers to produce verbal or written descriptions which account for what they know. Their knowing is in their action (Schon 1983). A further problem is that 'we do not have the disposition or the grammar for talking about the way in which we reflect on what we do' (Smyth 1987).

Lack of self-confidence

In addition, many teachers have been socialised into believing that, 'uncertainty is a threat; its admission a sign of weakness' (Schon 1983). They believe that valid knowledge about teaching resides in those outside schools and so historically have been inhibited from developing and articulating theory about what works in teaching which derives from analysis of practice.

In effect, then, there are two problems to be faced. The first is concerned with self-confrontation and the extent to which an individual can engage in this, and the second related problem concerns the extent to which the consequences of self-confrontation can be accommodated in thought and action by the teacher without assistance. Traditionally there has been a separation between those who know about teaching (usually to be found in LEA inspection and advisory services and higher education institutions) and those who do the teaching (the school teachers). The former have informed the latter and these have accepted, rejected or modified their advice, clothing themselves with a 'healthy cynicism'. Attempts to change teachers and schools which have originated from the outside have often met with resistance or rhetoric rather than a reality of change. This is particularly true of those attempts which have been under-resourced and failed to take into account that learning and therefore change, is a long term process.

> ... desirable as speedy and inexpensive changes undoubtedly are from a political and economic viewpoint, they are not likely to be easily attained, and strategies for change which assume otherwise are not likely to prove cost effective in the long run.
>
> (Bolam 1985).

It seems, then, that resistance to innovation may be caused because teachers need to maintain current systems, because of plain stubborness, or because they themselves have played no significant part in its creation and development. This issue of ownership is vital in planning for staff development, for if heads and teachers do not feel that the work belongs to them (in the sense that it matches their perceived needs and those of the school) then they may not be prepared to accord the extra time, energy and commitment necessary for its development.

So far it has been argued that the constraints on learning and change caused by the political accountability context are compounded by social and psychological factors. Formal appraisal will, for many teachers, be something new, an innovation, and as such will carry with it two elements which are potentially threatening to all but the most self-confident teachers – disclosure (to self and others) and feedback. Although writing within the context of innovation in American schools, Doyle and Ponder (1976) have much to say which is of relevance to the appraisal debate. They write of the possible effects of formal evaluation and the reduction of autonomy, increased 'visibility' and external control which accompanies this:

> ...the requirement for formal evaluation... increases the information flow surrounding participants' techniques and practices. However meritorious these conditions might be, they combine to increase visibility.... With increased visibility comes a reduction in the isolation and functional autonomy of individual teachers and an increase in external control over them. Innovation projects, in other words, generate a set of control mechanisms which are typically absent from the normal teaching environment. Such mechanisms increase teacher passivity and suspend normal teacher reactions to improvement directives...
>
> (Doyle and Ponder 1976)

It follows, then, that where teachers are not themselves involved in decisions regarding the design, process and use of appraisal *from the beginning*, then it is quite likely that this enterprise upon which so much has been endowed by Government and others in terms of finance, resources and expectations, will have a negative effect on teacher learning. In summary, *professional development will be hindered if appraisal systems*:

1 are imposed not negotiated i.e. presuppose that teachers are incapable of acting responsibly and autonomously;
2 address agencies, issues and concerns of someone within the administrative or bureaucratic hierarchy rather than the teacher or school (Smyth 1986) i.e. do not take into account the needs of teachers and schools as they perceived them;
3 imply a situation which is unpleasant, possesses threat, and typically culminates in unrewarding consequences (Withall and Wood 1979) i.e. do not arise from and encourage trust, commitment and confidentiality;
4 involve one group of people using technology and knowledge to do things to another group of people in a systematic and manipulative way i.e. ignore moral and ethical issues of autonomy and ownership;
5 fail to take into account the need for time for reflection during the school day;
6 fail to provide tangible support for learning after appraisal i.e. in-service as a built in part of the scheme.

The leadership factor

Effective appraisal, then, will need to motivate and involve teachers. It will need to provide assistance to those already engaged in monitoring their work – and it is the assumption of this book that most already do this informally – through resource support and further in-service training opportunities, and it will need to gain the confidence of teachers in its worthwhileness and 'practicality' in terms of their classroom work. Not all teachers, even then, will willingly commit themselves. There will always be the, 'stone age obstructionists' who neither accept the need nor have the desire to change (Doyle and Ponder 1976). In most schools there will be some teachers who are either:

1 frustrated in their ambitions;
2 happy to be in their final posts;
3 likely to gain (further) promotion (Hands 1981).

Not all schools will contain all of these extreme categories of teacher, but they do serve to draw the attention of headteachers and others concerned with appraisal to the complex web of role expectations, institutional constraints, professional experiences, teaching attitudes and approaches, and personality factors which may influence the responses of staff towards the introduction of appraisal into the school. Part of the conditions for successful appraisal is that schools and teachers need to be in a state of professional development 'readiness'. Relationships among colleagues needs to be open; there needs to be an ethos of trust and sharing in an activity which involves, as we have already suggested, not only disclosure of self but also opening up self to the possibility of feedback. Among the discussion of consideration, negotiation and implementation of appraisal 'systems', whatever their stated purposes, it is as well to remember that:

1 It is not easy to receive help.
2 It is difficult to commit one's self to change.
3 It is difficult to submit to the influence of a helper: help is a threat to esteem, integrity and independence.
4 It is not easy to trust a stranger and be open with him/her.
5 It is not easy to see one's problems clearly at first.
6 Sometimes problems seem too large, too overwhelming, or too unique to share easily.

(Egan 1982)

The implication of this for school leaders whether they be heads, deputies, postholders or other colleagues, is that their primary function is not to identify needs for others, but to involve others in identifying their own needs and those of the school by providing environments and kinds of support which minimize constraints upon learning and in which a variety of concrete individual and collective experiences may be reflected upon, discussed, assimilated and accommodated. It will not be enough, for example, to make organisational changes without taking into account the amount of support which those involved in implementing the changes will need, for change for this kind, 'will not persist if some individual changes do not occur; and changes in the ways individual professionals think and work will soon regress without supporting organisational change' (Schmuck 1980).

A model for promoting professional development

Below we have outlined one tentative model for professional development. It attempts to build upon the knowledge which we believe teachers already have, albeit intuitively, concerning practice, through a series of opportunities for conscious, systematic reflection which is supported in various ways by colleagues. (For a full consideration of 'action research' see Chapter 4.)

The 'intervenor' is not seen to be one particular colleague, nor is the intervention in the teacher's professional development at a prescribed time in his/her career. Learning is seen as a lifelong activity, though it is recognised that intervention in a teacher's natural learning cycle may be by invitation (related, for example, to a critical career development point) or by negotiation in the managerial interest of a school or LEA. What the model attempts to present is a learning support cycle in which colleagues from inside or outside the school may fulfil helping functions as appropriate. Help itself may be in the form of discussion, classroom observation, attendance at a course or other in-service activity, visits to other schools. Essentially, though, it relies upon the building up of a network of 'critical friends', and the success of this will be affected, to some degree, by the kind of leadership which exists in schools. Everyone is both a teacher and an intervenor, potentially a client and a critical friend.

Later we consider in detail the need for the positive and skilled leadership of interpersonal relationships in the school (Chapter 7) and some of the difficulties which may obtain if clearly understood distinctions are not made between 'professional' and 'personal' relationships with colleagues in conducting, for example, appraisal interviews (Chapter 6). However, it is appropriate at this stage to emphasise some ways in which leaders may provide appropriate affective support for teachers and colleagues. First and foremost there is a need for trustworthiness.

Confidentiality 'If I tell this person about myself, she will not tell others'

Credibility 'Interpersonal trust is defined... as an expectancy held by an individual or group that the word, promise, verbal or written statement of another individual or group can be relied on (Rotter, 1971)

Consideration in the use of power The assumption here is that the helper is perceived as having power and as being the kind of person who will not misuse it

Understanding The client can say, 'If I tell this person about myself, he will make an effort to understand me'. (Egan 1982)

Egan suggested a number of first steps in helping 'clients' which may be usefully applied to the school staff development context:

1 Attend carefully, both physically and psychologically, to the messages transmitted by the (teachers).
2 Listen especially for basic or core messages.

Figure 2.1: An interventionist model for promoting professional development

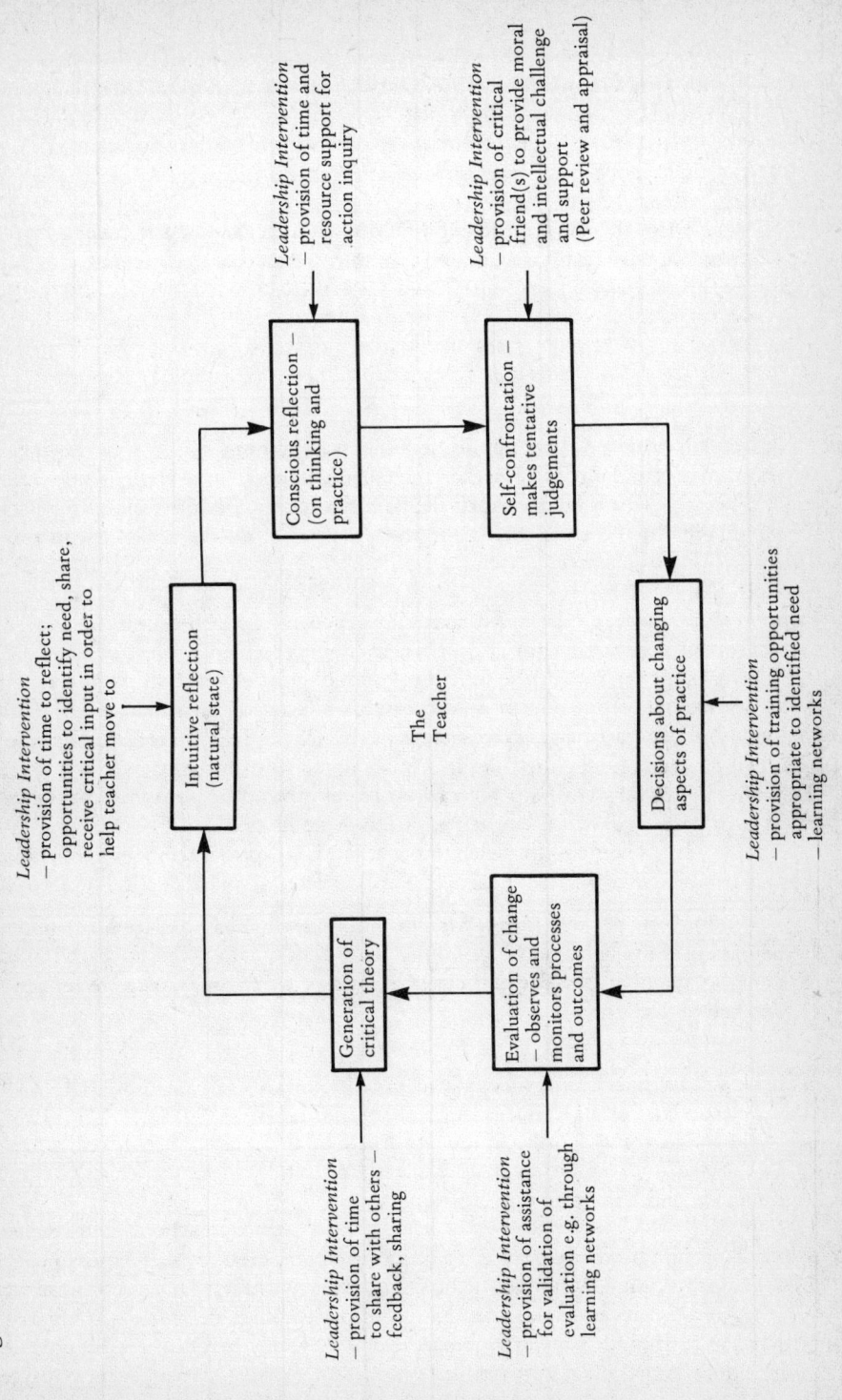

Leadership Intervention
– provision of time to reflect; opportunities to identify need, share, receive critical input in order to help teacher move to

Leadership Intervention – provision of time and resource support for action inquiry

Leadership Intervention – provision of critical friend(s) to provide moral and intellectual challenge and support (Peer review and appraisal)

Leadership Intervention – provision of training opportunities appropriate to identified need – learning networks

Leadership Intervention – provision of assistance for validation of evaluation e.g. through learning networks

Leadership Intervention – provision of time to share with others – feedback, sharing

Intuitive reflection (natural state)

Conscious reflection (on thinking and practice)

Self-confrontation – makes tentative judgements

Decisions about changing aspects of practice

Evaluation of change – observes and monitors processes and outcomes

Generation of critical theory

The Teacher

3 Respond fairly frequently, but briefly, to these core messages, but be flexible and tentative enough so that the (teacher) has room to move (to affirm, deny, explain, clarify, or shift emphasis).
4 Be gentle, but don't let the (teacher) run from important issues.
5 Respond to both feeling and content unless there is some reason for emphasising one or the other.
6 Move gradually toward the exploration of critical topics and feelings.
7 After you have responded, attend carefully to cues that either confirm or deny the accuracy of your response. Does the (teacher) move forward in a focused way?
8 Note signs of (teacher) stress or resistance and try to judge whether there arise because you have lacked accuracy or have been too accurate.

(Egan 1982)

Possession and sensitive application of such helping skills is by no means guaranteed in the holders or senior management posts in schools. And so they themselves may be said to constitute another potential constraint upon staff development. In the end, this is the most crucial of all the areas of constraint identified in this chapter.

More than ever before, schools need leadership which can both provide moral support for teachers who have sometimes become 'punch-drunk' by external pressures on the curriculum and on their own perceived professionalism; and intellectual support, so that the staff development policies which LEAs now require annually from every school may accurately reflect the particular needs of the individual as well as the collective needs of the school. It is, therefore, incumbent upon all who hold leadership roles in schools to identify for themselves and to seek help and support in identifying both areas of strength and areas for improvement in their own helping skills. Even helpers need to be helped.

Finally, what is being proposed in this chapter, is an appraisal model which builds upon current primary school practice. This 'horizontal' or 'dialectical' appraisal:

> ... is a convenient term for the kind of thinking which takes place when human beings enter into a friendly (meaning: well-intentioned, co-operative, genial and genuine) dialogue in order to find a synthesis, or when they engage in reflection and self-reflection...

(Proppe 1982)

This kind of appraisal acknowledges that practitioners are reflective and self-critical and that the goal of appraisal is not to simplify but to recognise complexities of teaching and learning in order to learn to create further possibilities of learning. In effect, it seeks to empower teachers rather than to disenfranchise them as autonomous and responsible professionals.

Appraisal must not be seen as a delivery of a service to schools and teachers which, by implication, are deemed to be incompetent, inefficient, inexperienced or in need of re-skilling. Systems which take no account of knowledge of professional learning and constraints upon this, change processes and leadership interventions – which ignore the need to provide conditions in which teachers are empowered rather than constrained – are unlikely to result in real, lasting change. Used positively, appraisal can be a means of encouraging teacher autonomy in which teachers become more capable of analysing and changing their own actions, using evidence and data rather than intuition or speculation as a basis to knowledge claims about teaching.

There are essentially two ways of viewing appraisal – as a delivery system through which to attempt to exercise more control of teaching, or as a 'form of empowerment by which teachers are able to gain tacit knowledge as a basis for transforming both their understandings, practices and the debilitating aspects of their institutional lives' (Smyth 1985). We hope that the appraisal adopted in schools will be of the latter.

3 The organisational setting

The key purpose of appraisal is to improve the quality of teaching and thereby to increase learning opportunities for pupils in classrooms. One of the factors emphasised in the previous chapter is the slow process of change in the ways that the learning process has been managed by teachers. The observations of HMI in their compilation of published school reports 'Education Observed' and the researches of both Joan Barker-Lunn and the ORACLE team based at Leicester University have suggested that contrary to popular belief the way that learning in primary classrooms is conducted is not very different today than it was forty years ago. Given such an unconducive climate for change what actual impact on the nature and quality of classroom teaching is the innovation of appraisal likely to have?

Much will be expected of appraisal, both from outside the profession and from within it. For those who have the responsibility for its introduction and its day to day management appraisal will make many and varied demands. One of the key challenges will be to the quality of organisational awareness that exists within the staff team and particularly in the head and the deputy. It is with these important factors that this chapter is concerned. It will attempt to place the process of appraisal within the context of a dynamic, human environment and consider the key factors and forces that affect the way that the staff of the school go about the business of organising and managing the learning of the pupils.

Much of the literature of educational management is concerned with organisational life in general terms, with ideas and theories that apply in all institutions. This chapter suggests that while such an approach is important it is also limited. What is needed here is an approach which helps those involved in the day to day management of a school to raise their awareness of the particular and unique set of factors which condition progress, development and attempts at change. While acknowledging the considerable impact that outside forces have on those who work within schools, the chapter will place emphasis on those internal regulators which exercise influence in unique and specific ways.

One of the features of the recent debate about how schools are managed has been a preoccupation with commonality and the striving towards a more unified and standardized approach in schools. This has tended to take the attention of teachers away from the factors within their own school which influence outcomes. One of the key features of any organisation is the coming together into a relationship of a variety of perceptual viewpoints. This can make the defining of an internal reality – what we believe in here, what we are doing and where we are wanting to go – very difficult. The tendency is to opt out of this process altogether. School brochures and curriculum documents set out a generalised ideology which can conceal, rather than reveal the complex and sometimes conflicting viewpoints that actually exist within a particular institution.

Having derived a generalised ideology, attempts are then made to work within it, proceeding on the assumption that what has been expressed is what the staff as a whole collectively believe. It is not surprising that innovation and change become so problematical. Until attempts are made to make the internal human and organisational forces explicit it is unlikely that progress can be made. This is not an easy task and given the sparing amounts of time that are available for staffs to tackle such issues, the chances of success may seem remote. If appraisal is to go even some way towards satisfying the demands made upon it then an increased attention to the internal dynamics and relationships within the school will be necessary.

It is vitally important for those who will be appraised to see their work in relation to the work that all teachers do in a national framework of expectation and evaluation. But it is also essential for them to see how their work in a particular school is itself a response to the nature of the organisational environment in which they are situated. The key concern here is to assess how this particular school with its specific characteristics and features affects the individual teacher's work and teaching performance. Those who will conduct appraisal will need an increased awareness of organisational features if they are to understand the context and background against which appraisal will take place. But more than this they will need the skills to help those they are appraising to gain it as well.

Within the context of this book the term organisation assumes a distinctly humanistic rather than mechanistic aspect. The school as an organisation is seen as a complex and dynamic network of human interaction and relationships. The central aims of schools should be concerned with human growth and development. It is the view of the authors that these aims can only be achieved in an organisational framework which is itself 'person centred'. If appraisal is to be successful it will need to facilitate person centredness, a concept which is further explored in Chapter 7. The purpose of this chapter is to offer ideas and perspectives designed to heighten awareness of, and sensitivity to, the essential human aspects of school management.

A model for analysis

To facilitate the process of developing a more sensitive organisational awareness, some sort of analytical framework is necessary. The framework that follows is an attempt to conceptualise aspects of organisational life which have a strong influence on the way that work is undertaken and results are achieved. It is important to remember, however, that such a framework is a mental map of a perceived reality, not reality itself. It can be used to gain understanding of the ways we get access to organisational reality, and provides us with a focal point for analysis. The model should be judged by its usefulness in helping to deepen understanding. Above all it should be seen as a temporary device, a tool for the moment to be tried out and experimented with in the human context of the school.

The model conceptualises the educational and management processes of the school as consisting of three sets of dynamic forces interacting within the circle which represents the boundary between external pressures and forces and the school itself. Although the model can be used in the wide context of a whole school, including all learning activities, extra-curricular events and pupil interactions, it is best conceived for present purposes as a model of the teaching staff and including all aspects of their work, individually, in small groups or units and as a whole team. It attempts to portray the interplay between three very powerful sets of forces, each of which needs to be understood if the business of management, staff development and appraisal is to be conducted successfully.

Although this chapter is concerned to raise awareness of the factors at work within the school organisation itself, it is important to recognise the influence exerted by external pressures and expectations. The boundary that separates the 'inside' of the school as an organisation from the 'outside' is in a constant state of change. Formally, the boundary changes as legislation restructures the relationship between the school, the governing body and the LEA; and informally as parental involvement and community education developments alter the relationship of the school to its neighbourhood. While organisational awareness demands perceptive analysis of the internal dynamics defined in the model it is vital to see them in relation to the forces that act upon them from the outside – public opinion, parental pressure, LEA policies, HMI reports and professional politics.

While the model can be used to consider organisational elements which are common to all schools, it is best used to grapple with the characteristics of a particular institution. Each school staff creates an individual dynamic profile which has aspects in common with other schools but which has something precise and unique. It is that preciseness and that uniqueness which it is so important to identify and come to terms with.

The model can be used to consider such questions as:

- How do values and attitudes affect relationships?
- In what ways do relationships express themselves?
- How is power and authority managed in the school?
- Which particular relationships affect the process of management?
- What are the key features of the psychological climate of the school?
- How do the fears and anxieties of individual teachers get expressed?
- In what ways does conflict express itself and how is it dealt with?

Such issues as these are at the centre of organisational life and affect the realisation of the aims and objectives that are being pursued. If such issues are ignored then it is unlikely that progress towards planned change will be successful. All of the questions relate specifically to the introduction and implementation of any scheme of teacher appraisal.

The organisational setting 35

```
          EXTERNAL EXPECTATIONS AND PRESSURES

                    VALUES
                     AND
                  ATTITUDES


         POWER              RELATIONSHIPS
          AND                    AND
        AUTHORITY            INTERACTIONS


          INTERNAL BEHAVIOUR AND COMMUNICATIONS
```

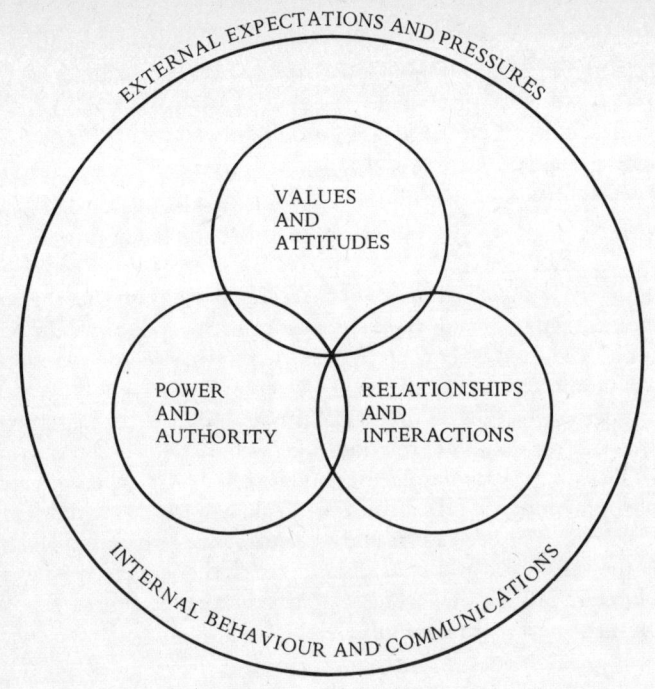

Figure 3.1: The organisational model

In Figure 3.1 above the three sets of organisational factors are equally distributed. Such tidiness and elegance is unlikely to feature in many schools. Each school will have its unique profile with the weighting between the factors varying as circumstances and conditions change and fluctuate. This is not to suggest that a diagram can adequately illustrate the complex interplay of forces that operate within any one school. What the model can do is suggest some focus points, offer particular lines of enquiry and provide a framework for institutional analysis. Let us now look at each of the three sets of forces in more detail.

Values and ideologies

The first of the key features affecting growth, development and change within the school is the complex network of value systems. While an individual teacher's work will be conditioned and largely determined by the attitudes, beliefs and ideas that are brought to bear upon it, the work of the school as a whole will be equally conditioned by the way that individual value systems relate and interact with each other.

To understand an organisation at work it is necessary to be aware of the various value systems that exist. This is a matter of attempting to tease out the ways in which the values, attitudes, assumptions and ideals of each member of staff contribute to and affect the work of the school as a whole. Each teacher can be considered as having a personal value system consisting of:

1 Values: specified and prized opinions.
2 Attitudes: more or less settled modes of thinking.
3 Assumptions: taken for granted ideas and opinions.
4 Ideals: high personal concepts and visions.
5 Beliefs: ideas accepted as truths.

Although as individuals we are constantly changing and modifying our personal value system, as we have seen in Chapter 2 we do so within a fairly fixed framework established in our early socialisation and education. By the time teachers take up their first appointment in school the central core of the value system has some stability to it. The surface elements are more open to change and modification as new ideas and experiences are assimilated. This value system has a powerful effect. Not only does it determine how an individual thinks and feels, it affects behaviour, particularly in relationships. New relationships are very much about testing out interpersonal value systems for similarities and differences. Clashes of values may inhibit the development of the relationship while differences of attitude may serve to extend or deepen it. The decision to end or continue an interaction will often be determined by the sense of comfort or discomfort that is experienced as the two value systems interact. Within an organisation this process becomes more complex but very significant. A new teacher joining the staff of a school will have a number of adjustments to make in terms of values:

1 To the formally expressed values of the school.
2 To the perceived values of the school as expressed through the behaviours of its members.
3 To the value system of each new colleague.
4 To the values system of particular groups, partnerships and teams.

This will result in the new teacher tending towards either engagement with those colleagues with whom there is a high degree of values commonality and disengagement from those whose values threaten, discomfort or arouse fear and anxiety. This process of adjustment will be negotiated by the teacher in a fairly low key and non-explicit way. Some compromise of values may be necessary to maintain politeness and a comfortable interpersonal climate.

In a long-established staff the situation is somewhat different. Relationships are likely to have settled into a number of patterns:

1 Intimate and enjoyable relationships.
2 Diffident but polite relationships.
3 Strained and difficult relationships.
4 Hostile relationships.

In a large staff all these combinations are likely. Where staff have been together for some time they will each have built a picture, actual or perceived of each other member of staff's value system. These profiles will condition relationships and determine interpersonal behaviours at both the personal and professional level. Consider the following 'overheard' statements:

'It's no use asking him, he never co-operates in anything.'
'Raising things in staff meetings is frowned on in our school.'
'I don't know how he finds time to do all that display work.'
'I really don't know how to help her.'

Values are very much the concern of each individual and it is not suggested that the school should in any way attempt to modify them. However they do have considerable implications for the management of a school. One of the important aspects of appraisal is to tease out those organisational factors which affect teacher performance. While clashes of values may have some impact on the teaching style of individuals they are likely to be a much more significant determinant of effective learning in relation to the whole process of innovation and change. Successful change and development depends very much on the active and involved co-operation of the teaching staff, working together through teamwork. To ignore the effects that the interaction of value systems can have on the life of a school is to make a major management mistake. The process of appraisal certainly presents opportunities to make the whole apparatus of values, attitudes and beliefs more explicit, and thereby facilitate change and development.

For the purposes of analysis, value systems can be seen as having two aspects – non-professional and professional. Among the non-professional factors likely to have an effect on teaching and school life are:

1 *Personal* beliefs about the self.
2 *Societal* about society, how it is run, institutions.
3 *Political* distribution of power, resources, rights and responsibilities.
4 *Current issues* e.g. South Africa, Drugs, Football hooliganism, Education, Child Abuse, AIDS.

The important point about these non-professional factors is that while they may not affect 'good' teaching they will have an effect when brought into relationship with the value systems of other colleagues, either because they are similar or because they are different. It is these similarities and differences which have the potential to condition professional activity.

Among numerous professional issues to be taken into account are:

1 Aims and purposes of education.
2 The 'good' school.
3 Assumptions about learners.
4 Assumptions about effective learning.
5 Assumptions about teachers.
6 Professionalism.
7 Teacher politics.
8 School management.
9 This particular school.
10 Other schools.
11 'The office'.
12 Advisers.

One of the challenges for those in management positions in the school is to create conditions in which individual values enhance rather than inhibit development. Perhaps the only creative way to do this is to make them explicit.

Power and authority

A vital factor in understanding the forces at work within the school is the structure and balance of power and authority. These two words are often used rather lightly to describe the legitimation of those with senior responsibility for the management of the school. Authority refers to the right bestowed in someone to carry out certain tasks and duties. Power refers to that person's ability or capacity to discharge that activity. Headteachers of schools have authority bestowed on them by the LEA and through the governing body. Nobody can bestow power other than those within the organisation who are being led.

This relationship of power to authority is an interesting one. Appointments to headships are usually made to the person who most succeeds in convincing the appointment panel that they have the policies and plans that are needed in the school and also the qualities and skills necessary to implement them. Yet schools have changed very little in the last twenty or thirty years according to the research referred to earlier in this chapter. In an article written in the *Times Educational Supplement* in 1983, a then primary headteacher – Angela Anning – posed the question why so many heads, three years into their first headship began to think about moving on in their careers. This 'three year itch' she suggests is to do with the fact that having spent the first year making alterations and improvements to the internal environment of the school – pot plants, book corners and exciting displays – and the second year attending to the writing of school documents and curriculum guidelines the headteacher arrives in year three at a 'Beechers Brook' situation. This is the realisation that despite all this effort, what goes on in the classrooms between the teachers and the taught has hardly changed at all. To affect this requires management activity designed to change fundamentally the way that teachers go about their professional business in their classrooms. For most headteachers Beechers Brook is too awesome to even attempt to jump. Chapters 4 and 5 will, we hope, provide encouragement.

Despite the fact that headteachers of primary schools have considerable authority for their work, very few have the power actually to deliver what it was they were appointed to undertake. Teacher autonomy in the classroom is a prized concept among teachers. Their authority is to exercise their professional skills as they see fit. While curriculum development has been regarded as an activity designed to bring about changes in the ways that children are taught it has failed to do this since pedagogy and teaching methods have not been part of that debate. Most school documents and curriculum guidelines are collections of aims, objectives and programmes of content. Very few bring programmes of learning and the teaching methods that should accompany them into any sort of a relationship. So while heads have been granted the power to initiate developments in curriculum content they have found that attempts to bring about changes in method and process have generally been frustrated. The view has developed among teachers that 'What I do in the classroom is my business.'

Heads have very little to back up their authority. They are seldom given the opportunity to make appointments, virtually never given the opportunity to move out of the school teachers who clearly do not fit in or whose teaching performance is inadequate and, apart from resorting to disciplinary procedures, have no sanctions to apply. This is not to suggest that such devices would be desirable, but to emphasise that the issue of power and authority within schools is far from the simple business of headteachers 'running' their schools. Recent trends have been towards a more participatory style of leadership and heads are now encouraged to manage through involvement of all staff and shared decision making. Despite its democratic flavour, this trend does not seem to have increased the rate of change within schools.

It is against this background that appraisal and staff development systems will have to be introduced into schools. If this is to be done successfully it will be necessary to be very finely tuned to the nuances of school management and to be aware of how authority is discharged and power managed. It will be important to know the extent to which management structures themselves enhance or inhibit progress and development. It will be vital to have knowledge of possible human obstacles discussed in Chapter 2 concerning why some teachers are open to change and others actively resistant to it. Some of the reasons will lie in the values and attitudes that have already been considered but attention will need to be given to the effects on all the staff of the particular power and authority system currently in operation.

Any power and authority system in a school can be considered as having two interrelated subsystems – one formal and the other informal.

The formal system

The authority of headteachers although prescribed in rules and instruments of government has often operated through a process of divine right. Headship has a prestigious pedigree deriving from the old public schools and supported by an entrenched traditionalism, so that headteachers today may rightly feel that they have the whole weight of the educational system behind them. While there has rarely been any questioning of the idea that headteachers are essential to schools and that their job is to run the school, the precise details of their work has largely been left to chance. Some heads have been boldly and radically innovative and they have usually come to grief in a system which seems to prize uniformity higher than enterprise. Despite enormous room for manoeuvre, with no laid down agreed curriculum, headteachers in British schools have found themselves bound by the power of tradition and by the clearly held set of expectations focused upon them by the educational system itself and by the public at large. So one of the key issues for the head of a school is the defining and sharing of a job description. It is vital for the staff to know how the head sees the job of managing the school and essential for the head to know how this perception is regarded by individual teachers and the staff as a whole. New contracts of employment with clearly specified responsibilities will do much to clear up this confusion which has traditionally attended the definition of the role of the headteacher.

The way that roles and responsibilities are managed will also be important. The headteacher has the opportunity formally to share authority through a system of incentive payments. The position of deputy head will also be a vital pivot in the system. In terms of analysis it will be necessary to be aware of:

1. How individual post holders perceive their own authority and responsibilities.
2. How roles are defined and described through job descriptions.
3. How other staff are involved in the formulation of job descriptions and role definitions.
4. How roles are reviewed and developed.
5. How procedures are adopted for postholders to conduct their work.
6. What happens when postholders leave and posts become vacant.

Governors are becoming increasingly involved in the management of schools and it is important to be aware of how this changing dynamic is affecting the professional life of teachers. If there is clarity of role and purpose the relationship between staff and governors is likely to be a creative and productive one but where there is confusion then stress and tension is likely to result. Factors to consider are:

1. Rules and instruments of government.
2. Formal governors' meetings.
3. The role of the staff governors.
4. Informal contacts between governors and staff.
5. Reports to governors.

The final aspect of the formal sytem to consider is that concerning the relationship of the school to the LEA. Aspects of this relationship which are likely to affect the staff are:

1. Communications between school and LEA.
2. Relationship with administrators.
3. Relationship with advisers/inspectors.
4. Formal LEA procedures.
5. LEA guidelines and policies.

It is very often the head alone who manages the relationship with the LEA. It is important that every teacher feels involved and active in this partnership.

The informal system

The informal system of power and authority is somewhat illusive and more difficult to define. Within most organisations some individuals, irrespective of role or status, seem to have a quality of personal power. They may be referred to as 'strong' characters or as the sort of people who do not 'suffer fools gladly'. Alternatively this personal power may refer to a quality of inner strength and calm. Much of the interactional dynamics within a staff team will be affected by the relative aggressive, submissive or assertive tendencies of the individuals concerned. Other factors to include in this category relate to roles and relationships not connected directly to the organisation itself – like a relatively inexperienced member of staff being a regional union official or one of the staff being a personal friend of the local MP.

The informal system also manifests itself in a number of other ways. These arise from the unique collection of individuals who come together in an organisational setting to carry out specific tasks and duties. The interplay between the personal and professional roles produces a unique 'culture' or set of identifying characteristics which are unlikely to be replicated anywhere else. These identifying characteristics produce implicit assumptions and behaviour systems within the school which are not readily discernible or understandable to outsiders. These assumptions and systems are expressed in numerous ritual behaviour patterns which may have no formal or rational basis:

- Who sits where in the staffroom.
- Times of arrival and departure from school.
- 'In jokes' – usually about school life and particular individuals.
- Dress and appearance.
- Roles and responsibilities on school occasions – fetes and school concerts.

Although illusive, such implicit systems can wield considerable power and the staff can unconsciously find itself reacting to issues and concerns on the basis of 'cultural' factors rather than professional ones. Rarely does the 'culture' become explicit. It sustains and extends itself through banter, jokes, innuendos, non verbal communication and at times by undue reverence for its importance.

Relationships

The third key dimension to be considered in developing organisational awareness is that of relationships. It is in and through relationships that the characteristics of an organisation are expressed. A great deal can be learnt about a school through observing the interactions of its staff. In *Education Observed No. 3* HMI observe:

> Good working relationships with colleagues are essential for all teachers, for professionalism in teaching is a collective matter, to a degree not always required by other professions. References to the importance of professional teamwork occurs frequently in school reports.

While good management is always best evaluated in terms of outcomes rather than intentions it is important to raise certain questions in the light of this comment by HMI. First of all what are good working relationships? What do they look like to the observer? What do they feel like to the participant? And how are they created and managed? Perhaps the most fascinating yet illusive question is whether good relationships are the cause or effect of a well managed organisation? In the previous two sections of this chapter we have considered how explicitness of value systems can increase organisational effectiveness and how careful attention to the handling of power and authority can improve staff cohesiveness and facilitate involvement and participation in the management of the school.

It is through relationships that the management of the school is done. In countless daily interactions, some exceedingly brief, decisions are made, ideas exchanged, possibilities explored, problems dealt with and concerns expressed. The following list attempts to summarise the features that would characterise effective teamwork:

1 Awareness
2 Warmth
3 Interactions
4 Communications
5 Intimacy
6 Openness
7 Authentic behaviour
8 Motivation
9 Confrontation
10 Commitment

Let us look at these in a little more detail.

Awareness

Staff who have a high level of awareness are tuned into the organisational dynamics of the school. They have a healthy respect for their own strengths and qualities but also openly accept their weaknesses and failings. They are sensitive towards colleagues, respectful and nurturing of skills and qualities but also tolerant and encouraging of their weaknesses. They are alert to possibilities, comfortable with change and expectant of developments. Above all they are aware of limitations, their own particularly but also those of other people. They know they constantly get things wrong but accept this as the way things have always been.

Warmth

This is expressed in caring and concern for colleagues, for their wellbeing, comfort and success.

Interactions

Teamwork thrives on interaction. In pairs, small groups and teams ideas are exchanged, information shared, problems grappled with, conflicts resolved, new initiatives planned and outcomes reviewed. These interactions are characterised by a high degree of informality with meetings being called at short notice, business dealt with, decisions made and action taken.

Communication

There is intense activity at both the verbal and non-verbal level. In schools where teamwork is effective teachers smile at each other more, laugh together, take time to listen to each other and get more involved in each other's work.

Intimacy

Staff know a lot about each other because they are interested and concerned. Personal issues and concerns are dealt with rather than ignored. Although staff may not see each other much outside school there is a closeness about their lives together inside the school and a genuine sharing of personal and professional journeys.

Openness

Staff are prepared to give themselves to each other in the sense of saying more about their inner feelings and emotions than colleagues might in other schools. In particular they are not afraid to talk about their fears and frustrations in their classroom work and in the co-managing tasks for which they have responsibility. Above all they are open to honest and caring feedback from their colleagues, they want to learn, to do a better job than they are currently doing and to become more effective in their working relationships.

Authentic behaviour

There is a strong relationship between inner feelings and outer behaviour. In other words if authentic teachers are feeling angry they will not repress the feeling but allow it expression and colleagues will recognise this as a genuine expression of that person's state of being. Such teachers try to be the people they are rather than the roles they occupy.

Motivation

In the school with effective teamwork there is a high regard for motivation. These teachers know that effectiveness results when needs can be satisfied. They are clear about their own goals in their work and aware of those in their colleagues. They are motivated by a positive and compulsive push towards change rather than a negative and repressive pull away from it.

Confrontation

In case this is all beginning to sound very cosy and too good to be true it is important to realise that effective teamwork is also characterised by a high capacity for confrontation and challenge. In this sort of school there are more arguments, more struggles and more negotiations than in other schools because the beliefs in the end results are stronger. Above all there is a high capacity for making explicit the causes of conflict and the associated feelings that accompany them. There is seldom full agreement on vital issues but when decisions are made they are supported by all.

Commitment

In effective teams there is a clear sense of purpose and a strong sense of vision. Team members while strongly committed to their own cherished ideas also have a close identification with the collective vision they have had a share in forming. Above all theirs is a commitment to the process of teamwork, to ways of working and a constant striving to improve these so that results and outcomes are also improved.

A further insight into the way that relationships can affect life in organisations is provided by the Iceberg Theory. This likens the staff of a school to icebergs in a sea. Just as nine tenths of the bulk of an iceberg is below the surface of the water so, it is suggested, are nine tenths of the people. Only the heads stick out above the water line, nodding and talking to each other in polite and distanced tones. Below the water line however the icebergs collide and bump into each other, sometimes with quite damaging consequences. In the staffroom the real business in relationships is below the surface. Dislikes, fears, mistrust, envy, jealousy, anger and frustrations remain submerged. What is needed is for the water level to be lowered so that these interpersonal issues can become exposed, be explored and resolved. The superficial veneer of niceness which characterises the interpersonal quality of many staffs is counter productive and sometimes very damaging to effective team work, damaging to the participants involved and inhibiting to the development of more effective learning for the pupils.

Developing organisational awareness

The introduction of appraisal into schools is likely to be one of the most significant innovations in education since the passing of the Butler Education Act in 1944. If undertaken systematically and well it will have a profound effect on teachers' working lives. As a major change it has, as indicated in the previous chapter, the potential to be seen both as a threat to professionalism and the integrity of teachers, and as a most important enhancer of professional development. Those who will have the responsibility for its introduction into schools, and those who will exercise its day to day management, need to be aware of the tension between appraisal as a threat and appraisal as an opportunity: between it being received as a creative innovation and a destructive one. Much will depend on how it is handled in individual institutions and how senior teachers, headteachers particularly, work to develop an awareness of the organisational dynamics operating within the school.

No consideration of the organisational factors can omit attention to the human dynamics of change. Something of the difficulties inherent in change were hinted at by Machiavelli in *The Prince*:

> It must be considered that there is nothing more difficult to carry out, nothing more doubtful of success, nothing more dangerous to handle, than to institute a new order of things. For the reformer has enemies in all those who profit by the old order, this lukewarmness arising partly from fear of their adversaries who have the laws in their favour; and partly from the incredulity of mankind, who do not truly believe in anything new until they have actual experience of it.
>
> (Machiavelli, 1552)

Headship and change

This sense of lukewarmness often greets a newly appointed headteacher taking up a new post. When heads come into a new headship they usually want to change things. Often this urge is seen by the teachers who are already in the school as a process of altering and modifying practice. Seldom is sufficient attention paid to the thoughts and feelings of those teachers who will be the focus and subject of change. If there is an insensitivity to these aspects of change then heads will often experience the resistance of staff to new ideas as a personal attack and come to see innovation and change as an issue of opposition. In his notes on 'The Fear of Change', Alan Coulson has provided an insight into the psychology of change which offers guidance to heads as they contemplate the way forward in their schools. This can be summarised as four key points:

1. Initiators of the management of change need to be aware that when change is suggested those involved in it tend to want to protect what they see themselves to be.
2. The way that individuals operate in their particular work situations has come about through a long process of establishing an identity in relation to the demands and expectations raised. They strive to satisfy their own work needs and the expectations of others with the minimum of uncertainty and anxiety. Pressures to alter this way of being tend to be received as threats to the comfortable continuity of living and working.
3. Suggestions that they change their way of doing things and their approaches to the professional tasks for which they have responsibility imply a level of inadequacy in their performance and this threatens the identity they have striven to develop. The natural inclination is to become aroused in the defence of the familiar and established.
4. Far too often headteachers experience this defensive tendency as opposition to new ideas and see their task as one of overcoming this perceived resistance. A battle of wills can ensue which is counter-productive to the developments themselves and to the professional relationships which are so vital to their success.

(Coulson 1985)

Much of this polarisation can be avoided if the following six factors are remembered:

1. When teachers resist change they are not usually working in active opposition to development and change but demonstrating that a threat to their personal and professional security has been experienced.
2. Headteachers need to accept this response as natural and inevitable.
3. A key task for heads is to listen to the experience of those involved in planned change and to seek to understand what is felt to be threatened.
4. The head needs to be deeply caring and concerned about what it is that teachers feel they are having to give up and to be seen as an ally in this process and not as an opponent.
5. Heads also need to help colleagues to protect what they perceive to be under

threat while moving towards new methods and strategies.
6 In the process of innovation it is vital to try and avoid undermining the teachers' sense of competence and professional well-being by appearing to reject or devalue their established practices.

Much pain and discomfort in schools can be avoided if some of these key ideas are incorporated in the assumptions which underlie approaches to management and leadership. A great deal of the stress within school staffs can be traced back to insensitive and clumsy handling of innovation and change. For the new headteacher, the careful application of the analytical model described earlier will help to assess the psychological climate and identify the range of forces which will operate both to facilitate and inhibit development. The introduction of appraisal will need the same meticulous preparation if it is to be successful in satisfying the hopes expressed for it. If there are deep wounds within a staff team then a clumsy introduction will reopen them. Raising awareness of these deep wounds and the patterns of behaviour which attempt to conceal them can lay the foundations for using the introduction of appraisal as a healing strategy, enabling old traumas to be exposed, apparent inadequacies to be disclosed and frustrations to be aired. Such an approach will do much to lower the water table and expose the icebergs.

Leadership implications

In their study of America's best run companies Peters and Waterman (1982) have pointed to a range of strategies which make for creative and effective leadership. With appraisal and staff development in mind it is useful to summarise some of these in terms of the headteacher's leadership functions in a school.

Management by walking about

Good leaders spend much of their time with the people. This suggests that heads need to spend the majority of their time alongside teachers in classrooms. They need to eschew the formal mechanisms of administration in favour of professional leadership focused on how children learn and how teachers teach. This will tend to help headteachers to be seen as partners in the educational process rather than as someone to be accountable to and who is one step removed from the real work of the organisation.

Use of temporary teams

School development and curriculum renewal is best facilitated by the extensive use of small teams specially convened to deal with matters of the moment. These can range from suggestions about end of term activities to a development plan for the design and technology curriculum. The tendency in primary schools has been to use individual teacher expertise to accomplish such tasks. Day, Johnston and Whitaker (1985) have suggested a variety of ways in which such a teamwork approach can be put to use in the primary school.

Promoting self-respect

Teachers work best when they feel respected and appreciated for what they do. The headteacher has a crucial role to play in facilitating the development of self-respect among the teaching team and for encouraging colleagues to recognise and affirm each other's efforts. This is particularly essential in an organisation whose manifest aim is the facilitation of human growth and development.

Accepting failures

Getting things wrong is inevitable. Unfortunately, schools have inculcated in both teachers and pupils alike a preoccupation with mistake avoidance. Fear of making mistakes inhibits enterprise and stifles growth. Provided that mistakes arise when efforts are made with good intentions then they should be accepted as part of the natural and desirable order of things. What should be developed, of course, is a capacity to learn from them through reflection and analysis. Those who are punished when they get things wrong will cease to be innovative and experimental and seek refuge in the traditionally safe and secure.

Tolerance of ambiguity

Heads need to move away from the belief that there is always a simple solution to a complex problem. Most difficult issues have complicated solutions and the mark of a good organisation is one that can cope with the paradox of inconsistency. Good schools are usually only good in parts. Provided that there is a healthy recognition among the working team of the comparative strengths and weaknesses of the organisation, then achievements can be celebrated and more finely tuned and deficiencies can be seen as challenges to be responded to. If it is only the inadequacies of the school that are focused upon in the management processes then low morale and lack of esteem is likely to result. If attention is only paid to success then complacency will inevitably result. Acceptance of opposites and inconsistencies will produce a balanced outlook, creating a healthy balance between challenge and achievement.

Permanency of change

We are now living in a world characterised by accelerating and inexorable change. It is no use sustaining the view that if we can just hang on then things will get easier. The schooling experience for children will need to be developed to take account of this feature of our lives and the management of schools will need to become more quickly responsive to new needs and demands. The best organisations are those which have the capacity for flexibility and the ability to proceed in a constant state of diversification and change. Clinging on to traditional orthodoxy will simply be a recipe for stagnation.

Taking risks

The good schools of the future will be the ones who have dared to take risks, to dream dreams and work for their realisation. Just as children learn best and make the biggest breakthroughs in their learning when they have the courage to reach out and experiment so organisations which have an acute awareness of developing trends will encourage such behaviour in those who have responsibility for development and change.

Conclusion

This chapter has attempted to suggest that the introduction of any formal process of appraisal to the primary school needs to be accompanied by a heightened awareness of the organisational implications of such an innovation. Such an awareness cannot be a static perspective but a dynamic process of relating the work that the school does to the social contexts of time and place. Appraisal will need to raise awareness of the educational process as it is practised in the ninth decade of the twentieth century but also serve to anticipate the emerging needs of the twenty-first century in which the primary school children now in our schools will live out their adult lives. This suggests that a key dimension in the appraisal programme will be one concerned with anticipating, estimating, forecasting and predicting. Schools which relate their learning programmes to the social reality of the present are failing their learners who are preparing for a quite different reality. While there may be significant elements of the curriculum which will continue to stand the test of time it is no longer safe to make this assumption.

One of the key assumptions upon which traditional orthodoxy in education has been built is that teaching in schools is concerned with the transmission of knowledge, knowledge that will remain valid throughout our lives. Alfred North Whitehead observed as long as fifty years ago that such an approach would only work if the time span of major cultural change was greater than the life span of individuals. But

> We are living in the first period of human history for which this assumption is false... today this time span is considerably shorter than that of human life, and accordingly our training must prepare us to face a novelty of conditions.
>
> (Whitehead 1931)

It is only now, half a century later that we are beginning to struggle with these novel conditions. Commenting on the problems and challenges that will face the citizens of the twenty-first century, Alvin Toffler (1971) identifies three key purposes for schooling:

1 The process of learning HOW to learn. Pupils need to learn how to access complex data and information easily but also how to manipulate it in a wide variety of contexts. They must learn how to discard old ideas and know when to replace them.
2 Pupils have an increasing need to be helped through the formal schooling

process with the increasingly complex problem of building relationships, an aspect of personal development traditionally ignored in the school curriculum.
3 Changes in the nature of society will multiply the kinds and complexities of decisions facing individuals. Education will need to face the problem of overchoice and pupils will need to be helped to take greater responsibility for the management and direction of their lives than ever before.

Appraisal will need to help teachers, both individually and in their working teams to grapple with the implications of Toffler's suggestions. Not only is it vital that the process of learning for pupils is transformed to take account of this future dimension it is essential that the management processes within schools also reflect them. In *The Networking Book* Lipnack and Stamps (1986) outline the key features of networking structure and process. These features are also very much the ones that those working in organisations will need to be aware of as we move with changing times. The institutions which have the foresight and capacity to incorporate them in their organisational systems will be the ones well able to enjoy the satisfaction of continuous self-renewal. A number of key features which can be considered in relating the structural characteristic of networks to schools as organisatioss are described below.

HOLONS
This is the idea that a school is both a 'whole' thing but also part of something else in the larger scheme of things. Thus the school with its particular pupil and teacher population is unique in itself but is also inextricably linked to the wider network of learning and educational institutions.

LEVELS
The school as an organisation has many levels and layers. There are participant levels – learners, teachers, parents governors; management levels – head, deputy, scale post holders; policy levels – school philosophy, curriculum, learning programmes; teaching plans and organisational levels – values and attitudes, power and authority and relationships and interactions. Awareness of these levels and the dynamics of their relationships makes for deeper understanding and greater social cohesion.

DECENTRALISATION
This is to do with the relationship between the whole and the parts. Too much reliance on the external bureaucratic structure of the LEA leads to lack of enterprise, individuality and initiative. Ideally the school will see itself as a self-regulating organisation within a network of other institutions. It implies both independence and co-operation. Many schools are experimenting with decentralisation within their organisational structures, placing more emphasis on task teams, delegating authority more effectively, sharing power and encouraging professional interdependence.

'FLY-EYED'

Like the fly whose one eye comprises thousands of individual eyes, so organisations 'see' through many perspectives. Many schools strive in vain for a single, uniform way of looking at things instead of recognising the inevitability of varied and sometimes conflicting viewpoints. A good school will cultivate 'perspectives consciousness' – the capacity to incorporate multiple viewpoints and value positions. Where such a capcity exists there will also be a tendency on occasions to 'see' with a single eye, to form in concensus around an idea or strategy.

POLYCEPHALOUS

Literally 'many heads'. It refers to the need for leadership. The good school will be the one where leadership is seen as a function of the whole team rather than the role of a particular named individual. A process of co-management will be the characteristic dynamic with the emphasis on the facilitation of processes rather than the control of them. Flexible schools will contain teachers who are capable of exercising a facilitating function in one part of the organisation and a followership role in another. Where there is a strong central core of shared values and beliefs multiple leadership will be natural and self sustaining. This suggests that headteachers will need to accommodate both a leadership and a followership function within their schools.

The process features of networks include the aspects which are described below.

RELATIONSHIPS

This aspect of organisational life has already been referred to in an earlier section of the chapter. The emphasis here is on the need to shift the thinking in schools from 'things' to 'relationships'. The school needs to be seen as a complex system of interdependent and interconnecting parts. In systems theory relationship is everything. Within the school organisational awareness will need to be directed to the parts of the structure and to the complex and ever changing relationship between them.

FUZZINESS

An ever increasing problem of school management is that of defining the boundary between the 'inside' and the 'outside'. The increasing involvement of parents in a process of consultation and partnership is blurring the line that separates internal from external concerns. This tendency to fuzziness is likely to increase as community education further stretches the concept and function of the neighbourhood school. In the flexible organisation there will be an open and loosely defined participantship and the boundaries will ebb and flow according to the needs of the participants and the consequences of external events.

NODES AND LINKS

Each member of staff in a school potentially is both a node and a link – a node when work is concerned with unique and discrete activity and a link when the task involves the setting up and maintaining of relationships. In schools there is often a sharp role distinction with class teachers occupying the nodal structure and the headteacher acting unilaterally as a link between all the parts. Increasing complexity will demand a redistribution of those functions with teachers taking on an increased linking function both within the school organisation and outside it.

'ME AND WE'
One of the factors inhibiting the more flexible development of the primary school as an organisation has been the fact that teachers spend the vast majority of their working life isolated from their colleagues. This has tended to develop a preoccupation with personal autonomy and independence at the expense of organisational consistency and co-operation. With no time specifically allocated for teachers to concern themselves with the management tasks of the school the role of headteacher has taken on an all-encompassing role. This has frustrated attempts to introduce more participatory management procedures and sustained a tension between the classroom based work of the individual teacher and a concern with the teaching team as a whole. It has been difficult to build a simultaneous 'me and we' dynamic in which self-interest and group interest are complementary and compatible. Far too often self-interest conflicts with group concern, thereby holding back progress and development.

VALUES
Values have also featured earlier in the chapter. The point that Lipnack and Stamps make in the networking context is that whereas in traditional organisations values have come to be seen as intangible and somewhat unreal within the network, a concern with value is seen as essential for human organisation and purpose. Within the healthy organisation there will be a more creative balance between the values of individuals and the values of the school as a whole. Peters and Waterman (1982) refer to this idea in terms of an organisation needing simultaneous loose/tight properties – a fairly tight central core of values to which individuals are committed but from which they are encouraged to experiment, challenge and take risks. Self-growth and collective growth become seen as mutually compatible.

Central to the successful implementation of appraisal is an awareness of and sensitivity to the organisational dynamics of the school. This requires a capacity to read the organisation in all its moods, an ability to tease out the relationships between the individual parts and between the parts and the whole, and it also demands the vision to set this process against a rapidly changing social and cultural background. It also requires a knowledge of ways in which teachers may be assisted in gathering information about their performance and that of their schools so that they may continue to grow professionally; and so that they and others can be informed of achievements and areas for improvement. The next two chapters, therefore, provide starting points for thinking and practice for all those involved in review and development.

4 Teacher and school review

This chapter provides examples of and commentaries upon some techniques which assist in self review and appraisal both for individual teachers and the whole school. The approaches suggested are underpinned by the organisational principles presented in the previous chapter. Our hope is that the techniques will contribute towards teachers' thinking and provide stimulus and practical help, where it is needed, to all those who pursue that process of systematic self- and peer-appraisal which has been labelled 'action research'. The emphasis throughout is on the processes of inquiry rather than its products; and the assumption is that:

> Teachers must be educated to develop their art, not to master it, for the claim to mastery merely signals the abandoning of aspiration. Teaching is not to be regarded as a static accomplishment like riding a bicycle or keeping a ledger; it is, like all arts of high ambition, a strategy in the face of an impossible task.
> (Stenhouse 1983)

Yet the acceptability, worthwhileness, credibility and effectiveness of the review for the teacher and school will inevitably be affected by decisions concerning who initiates, designs, implements and evaluates. The final part of the chapter, therefore, considers advantages and disadvantages of three other kinds of appraisal:

- appraisal which is carried out on behalf of the government or LEA e.g. by Advisors/Inspectors or Advisory Headteachers.
- appraisal which is carried out by a colleague or critical friend on behalf of the appraisee, i.e. peer appraisal.
- appraisal which includes views of 'subordinates' within the system, e.g. pupils' views of their teacher or staff's views of their headteachers.

Included in this section is a critique of the suggestions that the linking of pupil learning outcomes with teacher performance can be a viable option within appraisal schemes.

The task of embarking upon whole school review is ambitious, but nevertheless worthwhile where, for example, the purpose is to evaluate curriculum (e.g.

continuity and progression), classroom teaching methods, or communication systems. Although school evaluation 'demands a degree of openness which on the face of it might seem to threaten individuals' or small groups' rights to privacy, to keep their classroom practices within the classroom and school policies within the confines of the school' (Simons 1984) there can be no doubt that schools do need to present accounts of their work to the public. Nevertheless, we believe that excellent schools, like excellent companies, have, 'a deeply ingrained philosophy that says, in effect, "respect the individual", "make people winners", "let them stand out", "treat people as adults" ' (Peters and Waterman 1982). If these comments are to be taken seriously, then it will be clear that individuals and schools must continue to be the largest active stakeholders in their own appraisal. The issues are those of *access* to their work and *control* of the accounts of that work. We believe that the onus for accounting for the quality of work should be primarily with teachers and schools but that they must recognise (regardless of any legislation) the rights of their employers, governors, parents, children and the public to have access to accounts and audit them for themselves. 'The more the staff of a school feel collectively responsible for the school as a whole . . . and therefore to each other, the more they can feel collectively accountable to client groups, for instance parents and children' (Elliott *et al* 1981).

Schools would be wise, also, to consider seriously the advantages of encouraging their client groups to participate in their accounting and review procedures and this is discussed further in the first and final chapters of this book. There are a number of approaches to the review process which are readily available, and this section provides examples of some of these, together with critical commentary.

Approach 1: Checklists

Many LEAs have developed detailed series of questions which provide aides-memoire for schools searching for a structure through which to evaluate. Categories might include, for example, the curriculum, staff development, the school and the community, record-keeping and pupil profiles, and resources. Below are three very different approaches by LEAs in support of whole school appraisal and development.

Example 1

One of the best known of the 'checklist' schemes is *Keeping the School under Review* (ILEA 1983) and the main headings extracted from this provide an illustration of the issues which might be involved for the school and its teachers in undertaking a comprehensive self review.

1 The children, their parents, the governors and the community.
2 Teaching organisation – school staff – responsibility structure – non-teaching staff – staff development.

3 The curriculum – continuity – assessment – extending the curriculum.
4 Organisation and management.
5 The building and the general environment.
6 Questions for the individual teacher to ask him or herself.
7 Questions for the headteacher to ask.
8 The future.
9 The acid test. (Would I recommend a colleague to apply for a post at this school? Would I recommend this school to friends for their children?)

There are five major disadvantages with adopting schemes such as that described briefly above:

1 The questions asked are not all necessarily appropriate for a particular teacher or school.
2 The exercise is time consuming.
3 The evaluation is usually at the level of talking about the curriculum etc. rather than observation of the curriculum in action, and so is limited.
4 Since the exercise is entirely within the school (although in some LEAs an account of it is required by the governors and education committee) its authenticity and validity may be questioned.
5 Most checklist schemes do not build in provision for appropriate support for change where it is diagnosed.

In addition research suggests that little use will be made of LEA self-evaluation schemes, unless they are mandatory, and that in the latter case the results may, even then, not lead to change in the classroom (Clift 1982; Turner and Clift 1985).

Example 2

At least one LEA, however, has compiled an approach to school self-evaluation which provides both a series of challenging questions on all aspects of organisation, curriculum and resources, and, it claims, ' . . . a focus for discussion between the school and those external agencies but may be called upon to help in school review or curriculum planning.' (Northants LEA 1985).

The document poses key questions which are designed to assist both heads and staff of nursery and primary schools to undertake an 'ongoing evaluation of the aims, objectives, methods and achievements of their schools and as such be helpful to them in their planning of the school's development'.

While the broad categories themselves are not dissimilar from those in the ILEA document to which we have already referred, in the context of appraisal it is worth highlighting the section in the document on staff development. Here is one approach which recognises the responsibilities of the school and teacher for their own development, and which puts alongside this the need for support for this from the LEA and the need for an accounting within the overall staff development plan:

2. **STAFF DEVELOPMENT**
Have the following LEA Staff Development Leaflets been well discussed with staff and have the relevant recommendations been implemented?

No. 1 School Based Induction
No. 2 Staff Development in Schools
No. 3 The Professional Tutor in Northamptonshire
No. 4 School Focused In-service Education

2.1 School-focused In-service Education

Is there an annual programme of school focused INSET activity related to specific curriculum developments?

Does this programme allow for teachers to see good practice in other schools?

To what extent is this programme supported by contributions made from teachers, inspectors, college lecturers etc. from outside the school?

What arrangements are made for teachers who have attended courses to disseminate ideas and new knowledge gained from these?

2.2 Personal/Professional Development of Staff

Do all members of staff have the opportunity to discuss their work and receive at least an annual appraisal of it by the Head or a Senior Teacher?

What career advice is available to teachers within the school?

To what extent do you ensure that teachers have the opportunity for varied experience in terms of age groups taught, teaching accommodation and responsibilities held?

To what extent do teachers have the opportunity to prepare themselves for what might be the next promotion in the profession?

What arrangements are made for the induction of teachers

(a) new to the profession?
(b) new to the school?

What arrangements do you make to ensure that skills which individual teachers have developed are used and maintained?

2.3 Teachers with Special Responsibility

What criteria are used for the allocation of posts of extra responsibility?

Are the responsibilities clearly defined with written descriptions and well understood by the rest of the staff as well as the post holder?

To what extent are responsibilities changed to meet

(a) the changing needs of the school?
(b) the need for teachers to extend their experience?

What standing is given to scale post holders to allow them to influence the policies of the school through:

56 *Appraisal and professional development in the primary school*

>   support and advice given to other teachers?
>   control of resources?
>   advice given to the Head?

2.4 **Evaluation of the Teaching**
   What arrangements are made for the assessment of each teacher's performance?

   What evidence do you have of the teachers'

   >   effectiveness in the classroom?
   >   relationships with the children?
   >   responsibility within the school as a whole?

   What arrangements are made for the teacher to strengthen areas of professional skill which are assessed as weak?

   What procedures are used when you are asked to provide references for members of staff?

2.5 **Training, Development and Evaluation of Education Support Staff**
   What arrangements are made for the induction and training of education support staff i.e. secretarial/ancilliary?

   Do education support staff have clearly defined jobs with written descriptions?

   What opportunities are given to education support staff to extend their expertise within the context of their job?

3. **THE SCHOOL AND THE COMMUNITY**

3.1 **Information to Parents**
   What arrangements are made for staff of the school to

   >   explain school policy and the curriculum?
   >   exchange information and views of the school's policies?
   >   meet parents socially?
   >   give parents insights into what is happening in primary education both locally and nationally?

   What arrangements are made for the confidential transfer of information to parents or guardians on individual children's progress at school?

(Northants LEA 1985)

Approach 2: GRIDS

The most systematic scheme which focuses upon assisting whole staffs to carry out a self-review of policy and practice is GRIDS (Guidelines for Review and Internal

Development in Schools). This was the result of a project initiated by the Schools Council and developed in collaboration with fifteen primary schools in five LEAs and a University School of Education. Unlike the schemes already discussed, it provides procedural guidelines as well as 'prompting' questions. Initially staff are recommended to take a broad look at the school and, on the basis of this 'identify one or two areas that they consider to be priorities for specific review and development, tackle these first, evaluate what they have achieved and then select another priority' (McMahon et al 1984).

The key principles underlying the scheme are that:

1 the aim is to achieve internal school development and not to produce a report for formal accountability purposes;
2 the main purpose is to move beyond the review stage into development for school improvement;
3 the staff of the school should be consulted and involved in the review and development process as much as possible;
4 decisions about what happens to any information or reports produced should rest with the teachers and others concerned;
5 the head and teachers should decide whether and how to involve the other groups in the school, e.g. pupils, parents, advisers, governors;
6 outsiders (e.g. external consultants) should be invited to provide help and advice when this seems appropriate;
7 the demands made on key resources, like time, money and skilled personnel, should be realistic and feasible for schools and LEAs.

(McMahon et al 1984)

It is clear from these principles that the main purpose is staff and curriculum development and that 'control' and 'access' are in the hands of the school staff. Nevertheless, it is recognised that there is likely to be a need to involve 'outsiders' in school-centred work of this kind. Indeed it was found at the end of a twelve month trial period that schools 'would be unwise to attempt... to undertake wholesale review and development without external support' (McMahon 1984). Additionally, the project team itself identified the most significant principle as being the *consultation and involvement of all teachers*. The appointment of a co-ordinator was emphasised whose principal functions would be to provide moral and intellectual support as well as to be responsible for progression and continuity. Eight essential tasks were outlined for the co-ordinator who should

1 Try to ensure that the teachers and others involved feel that the review and development exercise is significant, that the consultation is genuine and that their recommendations will not be ignored.
2 Explain the process clearly to the staff at the outset.
3 Sustain pace and momentum by helping teachers to draw up realistic timetables at each stage and then checking that deadlines are kept.
4 Provide strategic advice where necessary, e.g. how to collect information, what criteria might be used for assessment.
5 Keep a check on what is happening at each stage and advise specific review

and development teams if they meet difficulties, e.g. if they cannot decide on a focus for the specific review, fail to meet deadlines, find that some of their recommendations are not feasible.
6. Contact 'outsiders', e.g. LEA Advisers, teachers from other schools, college lecturers, who might be brought in to provide advice and help at different stages or to organise training courses.
7. Try to ensure that the review and development exercise is both rigorous and systematic.
8. Make some evaluation of the effectiveness of the GRIDS method and whether it achieved what was wanted; the end of the first twelve months may be an appropriate moment.

(McMahon *et al* 1984)

GRIDS identifies five stages in a cyclical development process: (1) getting started – establishing the conditions for the review and development and appoint-

Stage 1: Getting Started
1. Decide whether this method is appropriate for your needs.
2. Consult the staff.
3. Appoint a school coordinator.

Stage 5: Overview and Restart
1. Decide whether the changes should be made permanent.
2. Decide whether and how to restart.
3. Restart.

Stage 2: Initial Review
1. Plan the initial review.
2. Collect information.
3. Survey staff opinion.
4. Identify priority areas.

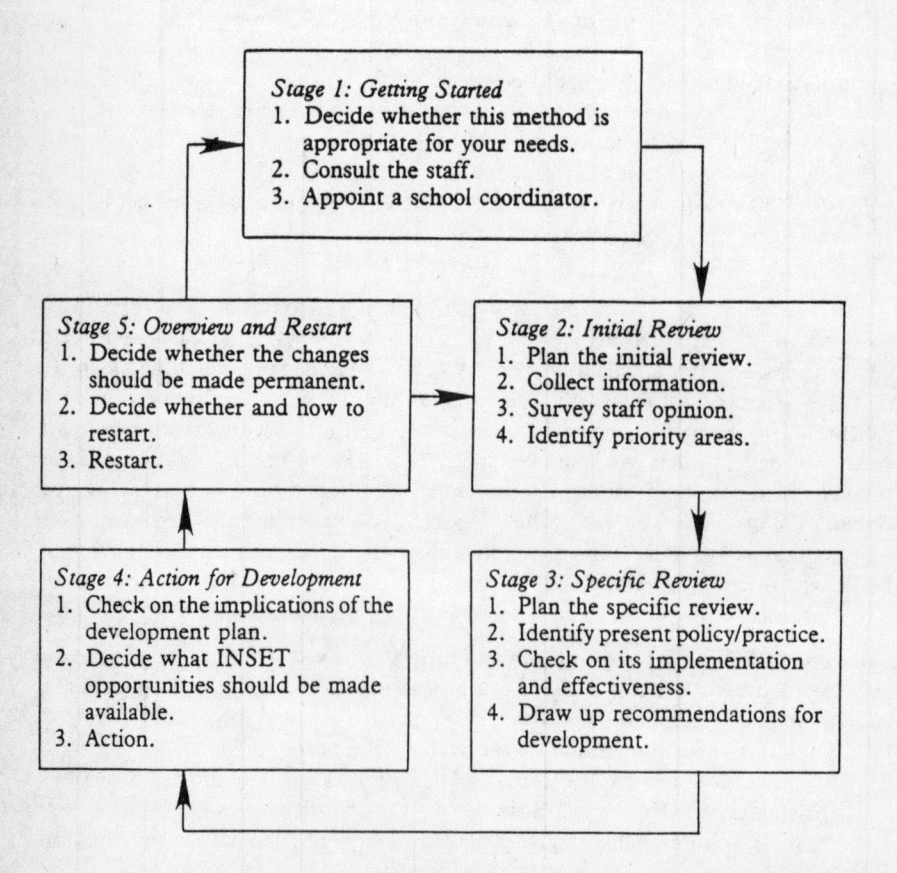

Stage 4: Action for Development
1. Check on the implications of the development plan.
2. Decide what INSET opportunities should be made available.
3. Action.

Stage 3: Specific Review
1. Plan the specific review.
2. Identify present policy/practice.
3. Check on its implementation and effectiveness.
4. Draw up recommendations for development.

Figure 4.1: The five stages of the institutional review and development process. (McMahon 1984)

ing a co-ordinator; (2) an initial review of work of the school in order to identify priority area(s) for specific review and development; (3) specific review of the area(s) selected as priorities; (4) development of the priority areas; (5) assessment of what has been achieved and selection of further priority areas. The intention is that one such cycle might be completed within a school year.

Essentially, the materials are intended as a do-it-yourself kit for schools. They may be critized as (1) promoting a 'top down' approach to school review and development, since it is usually the LEA or headteacher who initiates, promotes and provides support for their use, (2) being too clinical, (3) failing to provide advice on the management of change and (4) being unnecessary in small schools of up to four teachers where communication tends to be informal and where needs may be identified and met without a formal bureaucratic structure. Nevertheless, the materials do constitute one of the few comprehensive, documented aids to systematic institutional review.

Approach 3: DION

A further example of support for school-centred appraisal and development is through *Diagnosing individual and organisational needs for staff development and in-service training* (DION) (Elliott-Kemp and Williams 1980). This is a more systematic aid to the diagnosis of need – a first step in the appraisal process – at individual and organisational level. The scheme poses diagnostic questions for staff in school over a range of activities. There is an inventory of sixty-six statements to which teachers may respond and which encompass the organisation, the environment, and the perceptions of each individual teacher. The issues covered are aims and values, resources, staff recruitment and selection, organisational structure and roles, leadership, motivation, teamwork and conflict, creativity, problem-solving and coping, staff development and in-service training, and relationship with the environment. However, the authors state that before using DION, 'it is important to assess whether or not the climate ... is suitable for revising the problems and issues that it covers' (Elliott-Kemp and Williams 1980). Diagnosis is the first stage in a problem-solving process which is illustrated in Figure 4.2 (p. 60).

Planning Evaluation in your School

Table 4.1 (p. 61) simplifies the tasks needed in any evaluation into six main categories.

Conditions for success

Whether the scheme is internally devised, modified from one of those described here or others which may be available, each school must work at its own pace, must take account of its own priorities; and whatever the scheme that is adopted, it must be emphasised that the procedures should:

(a) be based upon clearly specified aims or objectives;

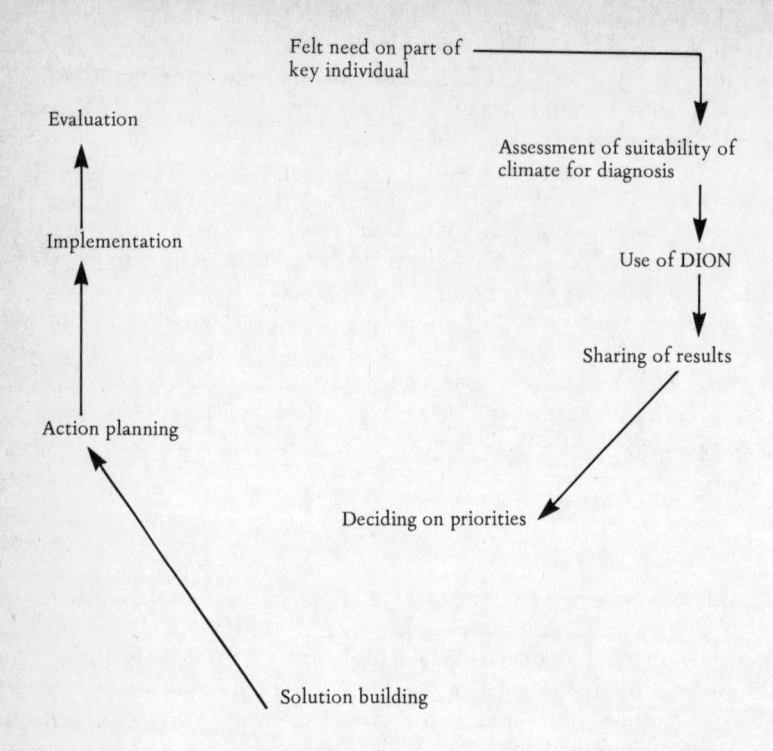

60 *Appraisal and professional development in the primary school*

```
                          Felt need on part of
                          key individual
  Evaluation
      ↑                        ↓
                          Assessment of suitability of
                          climate for diagnosis
  Implementation
      ↑                        ↓
                          Use of DION
                               ↓
                          Sharing of results
  Action planning
      ↑                    ↙
                Deciding on priorities

              ↖
                Solution building
```

Figure 4.2: DION problem-solving process (Elliott-Kemp and Williams 1980)

    (b) be adaptable to the differing requirements of individual schools;
    (c) provide information based on evidence whereby either
        (i) change can be justified, or
        (ii) the need for more evidence can be identified;
    (d) be capable of involving all members of staff within the school;
    (e) be operable within realistic time and resource parameters;
    (f) lend itself to obtaining the support and involvement of governors and the authority; and
    (g) lead to clearly identifiable pupil benefits.

(Schools Council 1983)

Schools Council Working Paper 75 (1983) suggests checkpoints or conditions for schools contemplating a programme of review, evaluation and development:

1 Gain the commitment of staff to conducting the programme;
2 Decide on the strategy and timing of the review and evaluation; in particular secure explicit agreement on the purposes of the evaluation;
3 Agree which members of staff are to be responsible for collecting, collating and analysing evidence;

Table 4.1: Planning evaluation in your school (Peacock 1987)

What do we need to do?	How could we go about it?
Regularly describe and discuss what we are actually doing in our curriculum area.	
Work out what are the most crucial questions we need to ask about what we are doing.	
Collect evidence that will help us to throw light on these questions.	
Decide what action needs to be taken, if any.	
Work out how to make sure that the necessary action gets taken.	
See that the action gets taken in the way we intended.	

4 After deciding which aspects of the school's work are to be developed, apply great care to planning what is to be done;
5 Ensure that all staff are kept informed of progress in the evaluation and development phases.

(Schools Council 1983)

These checkpoints imply principles of leadership and school climate, and a quality of interpersonal relationships which are further discussed in Chapter 7. Clearly, though, if such a scheme is to have a chance of achieving success then the head will have to be skilled in negotiating, contracting, and communicating with staff and able to supply the kinds of intellectual and moral support discussed elsewhere in this book. Table 4.2 (p.62) provides a summary of the conditions necessary if appraisal is to have any chance of success in school:

Table 4.2: Conditions for successful appraisal (Davis 1981)

Aims	Reasons
1 Familiarisation with the notion of evaluation	To gain and share information To lower anxieties To generate commitment
2 Establishment of supportive evaluation environments	To facilitate changes in attitudes, values, role definitions and self images To foster co-operation
3 Provision of physical and psychological space	To demonstrate support To provide time and somewhere to meet, discuss and work

Any attempt to initiate and sustain school and teacher self-evaluation must recognise what has been called the interplay between personal change, curriculum change and interpersonal change:

(i) *Curriculum change* is concerned with the *process* of identifying, defining and solving problems specific to the particular school.

(ii) *Personal change* is concerned with the *process* of perspective transformation – of seeing the world in new ways – which is often implicit in any real change for an individual. It necessitates:
  - reflecting upon our present practice;
  - challenging familiar assumptions which influence that practice;
  - exploring new ways of acting in accord with how we now view reality

(iii) *Interpersonal change* is concerned with the *process* of effective communication, so that mutual support may be sought and given through self-disclosure and feedback.

(Easen 1985)

A fine example of a source book which contains a series of writings and structured activities designed to provide experiential and reflective frameworks for coping with the *affective* challenges of school life – curriculum change, personal and interpersonal change – is *Making School-centred INSET Work* (Easen 1985). This provides information and practical advice on handling a range of human issues – counselling, feelings engendered by change, co-operation, conflict, creating a less critical atmosphere, classroom observation and analysis, problem formulation and effective meetings. In a sense, it provides a complement to the more clinical GRIDS approach and may be used alongside this. Like GRIDS it emphasises the need for a positive school climate in which there is affective as well as practical support for staff.

Whereas the first part of this chapter has highlighted curriculum change, the second will concentrate primarily upon personal change, and will discuss principles

Teacher and school review 63

and procedures for engaging in work which involves reflection, self-confrontation, disclosure and feedback. (Interpersonal change is the focus of Chapter 7.)

Personal change: The self-monitoring teacher/self-accountability

In the examples below teachers in one LEA met over time to diagnose their own needs and determine their own approach. The illustrations below are taken from this document. They provide starting points for heads and teachers to examine their thinking and practice and may act as aides-memoire for those beginning self-evaluation; and the questions posed provide, in effect, a list of criteria against which effectiveness may be measured.

The Teacher's self-evaluation

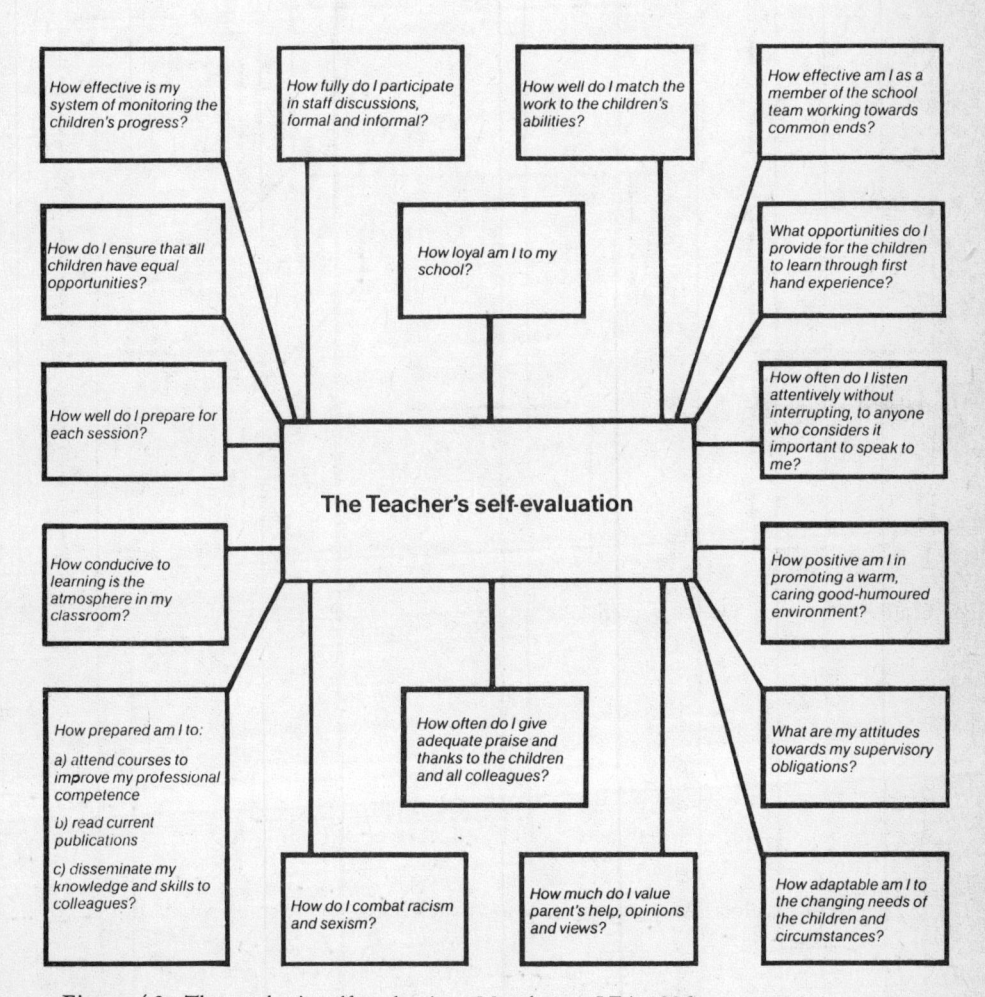

- How effective is my system of monitoring the children's progress?
- How fully do I participate in staff discussions, formal and informal?
- How well do I match the work to the children's abilities?
- How effective am I as a member of the school team working towards common ends?
- How do I ensure that all children have equal opportunities?
- How loyal am I to my school?
- What opportunities do I provide for the children to learn through first hand experience?
- How well do I prepare for each session?
- How often do I listen attentively without interrupting, to anyone who considers it important to speak to me?
- How conducive to learning is the atmosphere in my classroom?
- How positive am I in promoting a warm, caring good-humoured environment?
- How prepared am I to:
  a) attend courses to improve my professional competence
  b) read current publications
  c) disseminate my knowledge and skills to colleagues?
- How often do I give adequate praise and thanks to the children and all colleagues?
- What are my attitudes towards my supervisory obligations?
- How do I combat racism and sexism?
- How much do I value parent's help, opinions and views?
- How adaptable am I to the changing needs of the children and circumstances?

Figure 4.3: The teacher's self-evaluation (Manchester LEA 1986)

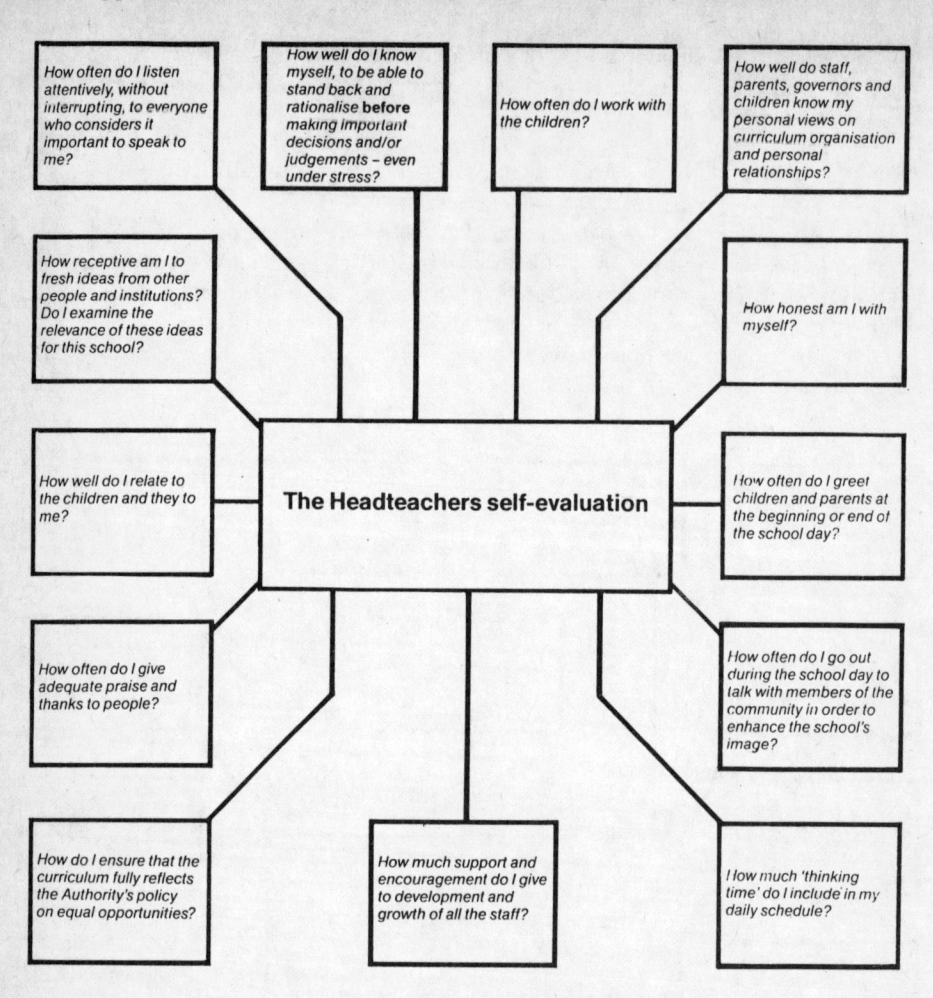

64 *Appraisal and professional development in the primary school*

```
┌──────────────┐  ┌──────────────┐                    ┌──────────────┐
│How often do I│  │How well do I │  ┌──────────────┐  │How well do   │
│listen        │  │know myself,  │  │How often do  │  │staff, parents│
│attentively,  │  │to be able to │  │I work with   │  │governors and │
│without       │  │stand back and│  │the children? │  │children know │
│interrupting, │  │rationalise   │  └──────────────┘  │my personal   │
│to everyone   │  │**before**    │                    │views on      │
│who considers │  │making        │                    │curriculum    │
│it important  │  │important     │                    │organisation  │
│to speak to   │  │decisions     │                    │and personal  │
│me?           │  │and/or        │                    │relationships?│
└──────────────┘  │judgements –  │                    └──────────────┘
                  │even under    │
                  │stress?       │
                  └──────────────┘
```

Figure 4.4: The headteacher's self-evaluation (Manchester LEA 1986)

Boxes around "The Headteachers self-evaluation":
- How often do I listen attentively, without interrupting, to everyone who considers it important to speak to me?
- How well do I know myself, to be able to stand back and rationalise **before** making important decisions and/or judgements – even under stress?
- How often do I work with the children?
- How well do staff, parents, governors and children know my personal views on curriculum organisation and personal relationships?
- How receptive am I to fresh ideas from other people and institutions? Do I examine the relevance of these ideas for this school?
- How honest am I with myself?
- How well do I relate to the children and they to me?
- How often do I greet children and parents at the beginning or end of the school day?
- How often do I give adequate praise and thanks to people?
- How often do I go out during the school day to talk with members of the community in order to enhance the school's image?
- How do I ensure that the curriculum fully reflects the Authority's policy on equal opportunities?
- How much support and encouragement do I give to development and growth of all the staff?
- How much 'thinking time' do I include in my daily schedule?

These figures represent a view of the most important aspects of teachers' and headteachers' tasks, and may be used in a number of different ways for different purposes:

1. They are excellent starting points and aides-memoire for self-evaluation by individuals.
2. They provide a ready focus for individuals to reflect on particular aspects of their practice.

3 They represent priorities as defined by groups of teachers. Other groups of teachers or whole staffs may wish to use these priorities as a basis for determining or testing their own sets of priorities.
4 They may be used in self appraisal as a baseline against which progress may be checked.
5 They may be used as means of sharing perceptions of practice with colleagues.
6 They may be used, as part of peer appraisal, as means of checking perceptions of practice against colleagues' perceptions.

In a sense, many teachers and schools already are involved in appraisal informally through lesson forecasts, pupil profiles etc. and formally through tests and teacher interviews with headteachers. Not only is this position justified in terms of teacher autonomy and responsibility, but it is also of practical benefit. After all, no matter what system of appraisal is devised it must take into account teacher and school contexts and the inevitable inclusion of appraisal of classroom and school work from the outside is bound to be temporary and partial, if only because of resource constraints.

We have argued, however (Chapter 2), that it is difficult to move from reflection (which may lead to the identification of need) to action (which may lead to change) without the provision of time and a framework for further action and support. The next part of this chapter describes one such framework for action which upholds teachers' professionality through the promotion of 'self-accountability' by means of 'action research' which should, we believe, form the basis of any appraisal system which is adopted by LEAs and schools.

Action research

Self-reporting, then, may be used as part of a system of accountability which 'both respects the professional autonomy of teachers and their right to dialogue with the public about their responsibilities' (Elliott 1979). The system might have three main features:

1 A school and its teachers would acknowledge accountability to their public by producing their own self-evaluation reports for public scrutiny and discussion. As a check against bias they could incorporate discussion with external evaluation consultants who had free access to classrooms and the school.
2 A school and its teachers would self-evaluate in the light of their own conceptions of the sort of things they are accountable for, but the evaluation reports should make these criteria clear and indicate a willingness to enter into dialogue with their public about them. Such an indication might involve incorporating into reports questions and issues about the criteria which are raised by the external evaluation consultants.
3 A school and its teachers would accept responsibility for establishing contexts in which genuine discussion and dialogue could take place and procedures for formulating and adapting policy as a result.

We have established in previous chapters that most teachers engage in self-evaluation as a natural and necessary part of, at the least, survival and, more often, ensuring professional effectiveness in the classroom, but that there are a variety of constraints which act upon this and that what teachers learn from self-evaluation itself is rarely shared or made public. Action research which is linked to self- and peer-evaluation helps to minimise (but not eliminate) these constraints and provides a framework for sharing. It may, therefore, be used as a part of an appraisal process provided that the purpose is primarily professional development. The process itself may, however, involve peers and others from outside the school.

Action research has been defined as the, 'study of a social situation with a view to improving the quality of action within it' and as providing, 'the necessary link between self-evaluation and professional development' (Elliott 1981). It is a form of self-reflective inquiry and its concern is to 'promote improvement in practice and improvement in understanding simultaneously' (McCormick and James 1983). Carr and Kemmis (1986) gives the following aims:

> There are two essential aims of all action research: to *improve* and to *involve*. Action research aims at improvement in three areas: firstly, the improvement of a *practice;* secondly, the improvement of the *understanding* of the practice by its practitioners; and thirdly, the improvement of the *situation* in which the practice takes place. The aim of *involvement* stands shoulder to shoulder with the aim of *improvement*. Those involved in the practice being considered are to be involved in the action research process in all its phases of planning, acting, observing and reflecting. As an action research project develops, it is expected that a widening circle of those affected by the practice will become involved in the research process.

Action research is at its most effective when carried out collaboratively, although often it is pursued by individuals in a school, sometimes with the co-operation of outsiders. It is increasingly employed in school-centred professional and curriculum development activities.

While this movement originated in America, it has grown in England in the last twenty-five years largely through the efforts of Lawrence Stenhouse (1975 and 1979), John Elliott (1975; 1981) and in Australia through the work of Kemmis *et al* (1981) who describe the process of action research as follows:

> In practice, the process begins with a *general idea* that some kind of improvement or change is desirable. In deciding just where to begin in making improvements, one decides on a *field of action*... where the battle (not the whole war) should be fought. It is a decision on where it is possible to have an impact. The general idea prompts a *'reconnaissance'* of the circumstances of the field, and fact-finding about them. Having decided on the field and made a preliminary reconnaissance, the action researcher decides on a general plan of action. Breaking the general plan down into achievable steps, the action researcher settles on *the first action step*. Before taking this first step the action researcher becomes more circumspect, and devises a way of *monitoring* the effects of the first action step. When it is possible to maintain fact-finding by monitoring the

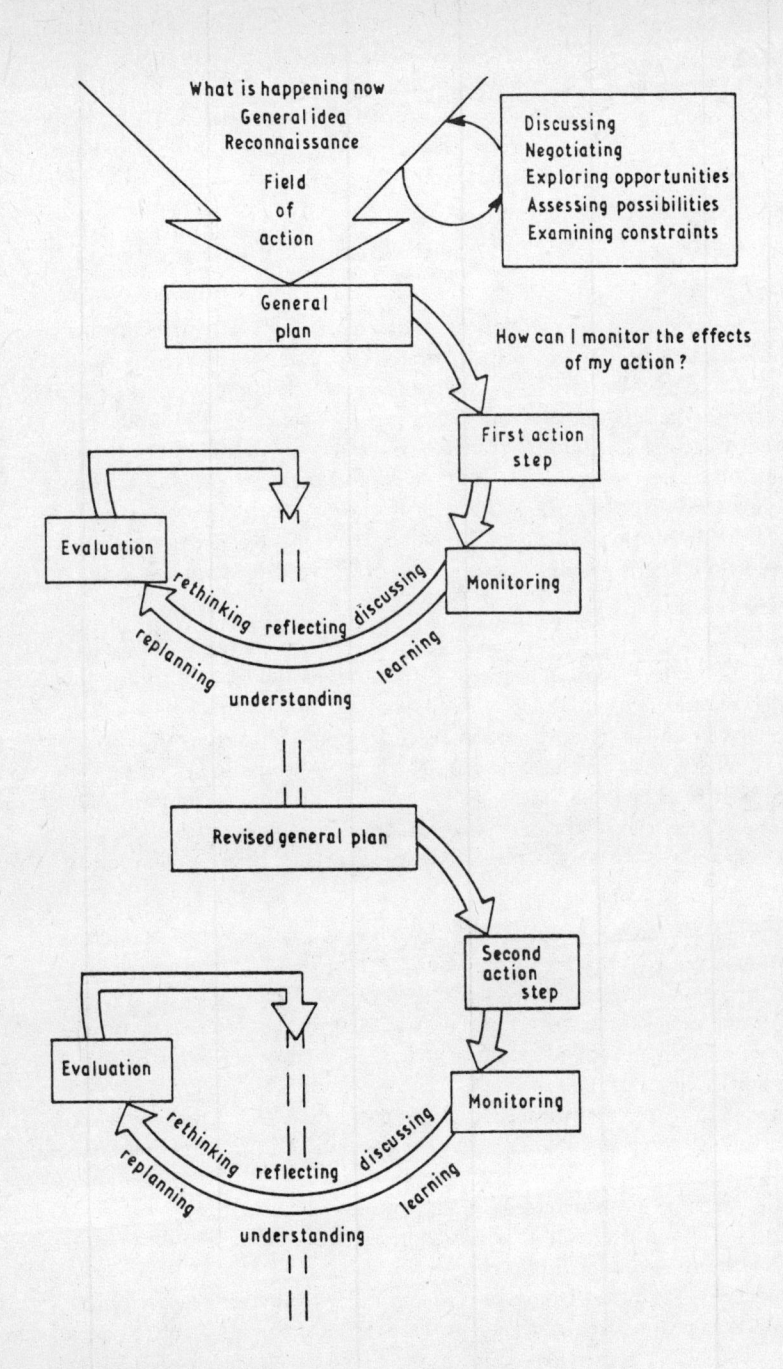

Figure 4.5: The action research spiral (Kemmis et al 1981)

action, the first step is taken. As the step is implemented, new data starts coming in and the effects of the action can be described and *evaluated*. The general plan is then revised in the light of the new information about the field of action and the second action step can be planned along with the appropriate monitoring procedures. The second action step is then implemented, monitored and evaluated; and the spiral of action, monitoring, evaluation and replanning continues.

Elliott sees similarities between this and the Aristotelian idea of deliberative enquiry:

> First, it is concerned with the developing of strategies for realizing educational values which cannot be clearly defined in advance, and independently of, the chosen means. Secondly, it is a process in which practitioners accept responsibility for reflection, and do not simply depend on the analyses of external investigators. The outside researcher's role is to stimulate reflection by practitioners, and the former's 'accounts' or 'hypotheses' are only validated in dialogue with the latter. Thirdly, and as a consequence of the above points, action-research always proceeds from the perspective of the practitioners' ends-in-view. And finally, it is a necessary condition of the professional development of teachers.
>
> (Elliott 1983)

He argues that the 'general idea' in Figure 4.5 should be allowed to shift and that 'reconnaissance' should involve analysis in addition to fact finding.

Some problems in engaging with action research – which is, after all, a way of describing how what many teachers do intuitively may be made systematic and explicit – were identified by John Elliott (1984) as a result of involvement in a DES Regional Course. These were expressed as hypotheses, and at least six of these are significant in relation to the classroom action research related to self evaluation and appraisal.

1. If the teacher-researcher's normal workload is reduced in ways which increase the workload of other teachers a 'boomerang' effect will occur when it comes to securing their co-operation in getting access to data.
2. Collaborative programmes of action research are unlikely to be sustained in schools when they are given a low priority at the levels of either school or department policy.
3. Teachers are unlikely to commit themselves to action research in their schools if commitment receives little recognition or reward from 'senior management'.
4. Initial research aspirations remain unfulfilled when teachers receive no allocation of 'bounded time', in which they are free to set aside other commitments to give priority to research.
5. A common cause of failure by teachers to implement an action research plan is that it tends to be overambitious and unrealistic both with respect to scale and to the methods and techniques employed.
6. Teacher-researchers in schools tend to opt for quantitative methods of data

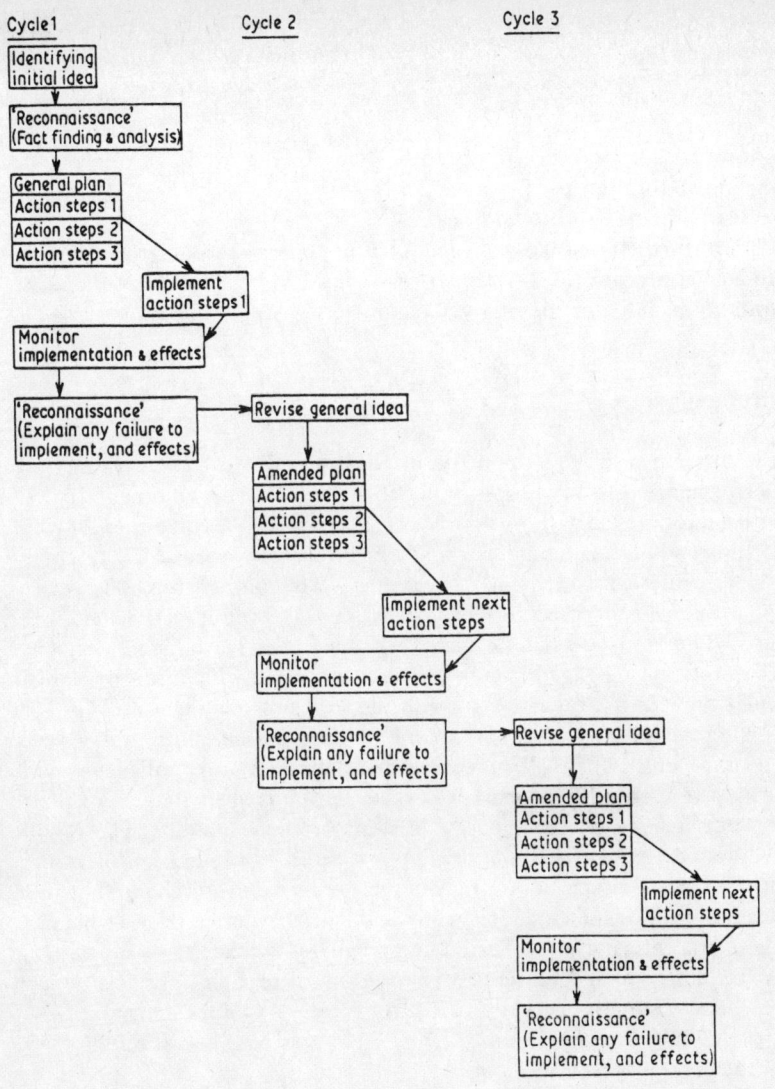

Figure 4.6: Action research as a spiral staircase (Elliott, 1981)

collection – questionnaires and objective tests – rather than qualitative methods – naturalistic observation and interview – because the latter involve 'personalised' situations in which the colleagues and pupils observed or interviewed find it difficult to mentally divorce a person's position and role as researcher from his/her other positions and roles within the school.

(Elliott 1984)

While these hypotheses referred to the responses of teachers who had been involved in action research as part of an in-service course/activity they are equally appropriate for teachers and headteachers who wish to pursue action research as a part of a policy for self evaluation and appraisal. They imply that:

1 Classroom research needs to be part of an agreed school policy for self-evaluation and appraisal.
2 Recognition of its importance needs to be given by the head and one way of achieving this is through the provision of time.
3 Action research plans need to be practical.
4 Where action research involves colleagues being in the classroom, this needs to be carefully planned and negotiated so that roles can be clarified and agreed. Confidentiality of information is a key factor here.

Appraisal from above

So far this chapter has focused upon the implications for teacher learning and change of performance review which is linked to professional development. In this sense, it has been concerned with *formative evaluation* which involves monitoring ongoing teaching and has as its main purposes the provision of feedback to teachers in order to help professional growth and enhance classroom teaching. However, those with management responsibilities for the system as a whole – DES and LEAs in particular – will wish to determine the overall quality of teachers and schools. They will therefore also engage in *summative evaluation* in which information is collected which might be used as a basis for informed decision making in areas of, for example, 'hiring and firing, promotion and tenure, assignments and salary' (Stiggins and Bridgeford 1984). Whereas headteachers and other colleagues will normally be involved centrally in formative evaluations, it is likely that they will be involved at most in an advisory capacity in summative evaluations. These will usually be initiated and carried out by an inspector from local or national government. This raises issues, not only about teacher learning and change but also about what criteria will be used to judge, who decides on these criteria, and what use will be made of the information collected and judgements made.

One LEA has designed and implemented a system of teacher appraisal which allows for teachers to request visits by an LEA Inspector who helps them to begin to answer the question, 'How am I doing?'. The scheme is based on the following 'rights' of employers, teachers and pupils:

1 That the employer has a right to know about performance in schools.
2 That teachers have a right to know what is written about them.
3 That teachers have a right to expect a programme of professional development.
4 That employers have a right to expect teachers to improve their skills.
5 That teachers should be involved in negotiating the criteria by which their performance might be judged.
6 That teachers generally wish to improve.
7 That the local authority should enable teachers to take part in the appraisal system.

8 That teachers have the right of access to skilled, informed and sensitive professional guidance and counselling.
9 That students have a right to well qualified and skilled teachers.
10 That teachers have a right to expect feedback on observed performance.
11 That teachers have a right of appeal.
12 That performance appraisal should eventually be managed in schools by school staff.

(Berridge 1986)

The appraisal system consists of one or more pre-observation visits during which the processes, purposes and use of the profile is explained and the assessment procedures agreed. A number of lessons are observed 'which represent the variety of work undertaken by the appraisee'. The appraisor completes a draft report and this is negotiated with the appraisee. Eventually, an agreed version emerges which is signed by both parties, then lodged for two years only on the teacher's personal file with a copy for the appraisee. The report is not used as a reference unless at the request of the appraisee. Classroom practice is judged according to the following set of criteria:

1 Preparation;
2 Knowledge of content;
3 Use of resources;
4 Organisation of work;
5 Classroom management and environment;
6 Relationships with pupils;
7 Pupil participation;
8 Questioning techniques;
9 Control/Discipline;
10 Assessment of pupils' work;
11 Lesson content and task match.

There is a section on the report for general remarks and advice given.

For the teacher who is practised in the skills of classroom observation and inquiry this kind of approach, based as it is upon negotiated contracts, holds no threat. On the contrary, it will provide additional means of testing and validating of his/her own work and that of colleagues. However, the teacher who is unused to discussion of jointly observed classroom data with colleagues or who habitually operates at an intuitive level may find it difficult to negotiate meaningfully with a relative stranger who is 'in authority'. Indeed, the process of negotiation itself implies the possession and application of skills which will be either undeveloped or underdeveloped in many teachers. Additionally, the effective implementation of such schemes as that described above implies that the advisory and inspection services are filled with people who are themselves skilled in the arts of negotiation, counselling and classroom inquiry. This is itself open to question.

So far, we have established that where inspectors and others from outside the teachers' immediate classroom and school contexts conduct appraisal, the criteria which are used must be made explicit, be understood and agreed as fair, relevant, valid and practical by teachers if they are to be perceived by them as being significant to their professional development. This implies a commitment of time to the process, and an ability on the part of the appraisors to establish trust, confidence and credibility over the relatively brief periods during which they and the appraisees are together. Even then, however, there may be problems concerning which criteria should be selected and how assessments of teachers and teaching are to be made.

The use of predetermined criteria

HMI (1985) state that assessment, 'implies the use of measurement and/or grading based on known criteria'. Thus it would seem reasonable for performance review to focus upon any or all of the following:

- teaching skills and qualities;
- professional and curriculum development;
- extra-curricular activities;
- management responsibilities and skills;
- interpersonal relationships.

Each of these categories may be extended and detailed lists of criteria may be made. There have been numerous attempts to define the essential skills and qualities of 'good' teachers and 'good' teaching. For example, probationary teachers should be assessed on the basis of 'class management, relevant subject expertise, appropriate teaching skills, adequacy of lesson preparation, use of resources, understanding the needs of pupils, ability to establish appropriate relationships with colleagues...' (DES 1/83). Many of those engaged in initital training assess their students through detailed lists of criteria relating to classroom competencies; and in discussing the appraisal of staff development programmes Downes (1984) lists the following as being desirable criteria:

> Commitment; leadership; standards of work received; self-presentation; response to colleagues' problems; motivating influences; sensitivity; tolerance to stress; standards of work presentation; classroom expectation; relationships with colleagues; chairmanship; career ambition; creativity; administrative skills
> (Downes 1984)

To these might be added others, such as reliability, loyalty, determination, initiative, relationship with parents, children and the community. *The point here is that what is assessed will depend upon the value systems of those who devise the criteria, the meanings which are assigned to them, the particular teachers' roles within the school and, where classroom observation occurs, the particular teaching and learning contexts.* The temptation for 'managers' who wish to take an overview of their workforce will be to adopt or devise a single set of criteria which can be applied to all members of that workforce in order to judge its effectiveness and to use the results to make comparisons between teachers and schools. Despite the obvious attractions of such schemes in terms of administrative convenience and operational efficiency, we believe that the temptation must be avoided.

Detailed examples of various checklist approaches can be found in the appendices of the Graham Report (1985), and these concern both classroom performance and the teacher's planning, development and contributions to school and community. In effect, they represent attempts to quantify what is essentially a set of qualitative activities. While they are useful as aids to appraisal their limitations must be recognised. It is impossible to assign a grade or mark to a particular skill or quality; and it is difficult to determine whether 'knowledge content', for example, should be accorded more importance in a lesson than 'pupil participation' without an understanding and knowledge of teaching intentions and the teaching and learning contexts of individual classrooms and schools. These are but some of the factors which may affect teachers' performance. Users of checklists and rating scales must take these into account, and gather information over a period of time. Unless performance criteria are understood by and agreed with each teacher and school, then the assigning of marks or grades for teachers will become part of an appraisal system which serves the need of administrative regulation rather than professional development.

The use of a colleague or 'critical friend' (peer appraisal)

So far we have argued that ideally both the criteria and methods of appraisal should be agreed with teachers if they are going to commit themselves to the kinds of review and target setting which will inevitably form a part of a school's staff development policy (see Chapter 8; see also Chapter 6 for a discussion of the appraisal interview). One obvious means of pursuing this ideal in practice is to involve groups of teachers in deciding upon which general or particular aspects of their professional lives should be appraised and the criteria which should be used to judge their effectiveness. This might be achieved with one or more 'critical friends'. In the context of the organisational climate and interpersonal relationships described in Chapters 3 and 7, peer appraisal is an essential part of the principle of collegiality. There can be little doubt that it is important to link in at some point with a colleague – the least threatening way is to exchange classes in order to check on your colleagues' interpretations of events. They will recognise that it is a snapshot of events which is being captured, so that, unless there are regular visits and exchanges, no attempts will be made to generalise. Dean (1983) suggests that *skills in observation* need to be improved and that one way of achieving this is through *working with colleagues:*

> ... skill in observation is one of the most important skills a teacher can have and it is a skill which teachers need to be working to improve all the time. One way of improving observation is to look at children and their work with other teachers, who, because they are different people, will see differently from you and may thus enlarge your seeing ...
>
> (Dean 1983)

This suggestion of bringing a colleague into the classroom to assist in the process of self-evaluation reinforces the discussion of professional learning needs in previous chapters. Just as important, it also provides, potentially, a means for teachers to validate their own interpretations and judgements of classroom action. In this sense it may serve the purposes of both professional and moral accountability.

This means that at some stage (and preferably at regular intervals) teachers should be encouraged to invite colleagues or 'trusted others' into their classroom for the purposes of:

1 Assisting them in the collection of appropriate information which will be helpful in inquiring into their teaching and their pupils' learning generally or a particular agreed aspect of this (a monitoring function).
2 Providing a 'third eye' in order to help them test the validity of their own interpretations and judgements of the teaching and learning in their classroom (an evaluation function).

These functions may, of course, be combined. However, it is important that they are mutually agreed. The outsider in the classroom is an advantage and from time to time necessary, in order:

1 to establish and sustain a responsive, mutually acceptable dialogue about classroom events and their context;
2 to audit the process rather than the product of possibly biased reporting;
3 to create a situation in which the teacher is obliged to reflect. This is unlikely to happen in the crowded school day;
4 to act as a resource which the teacher may use at times appropriate to the needs which he or she perceives;
5 to relieve the teacher of the need to gather his or her own evidence.

If one is on one's own, 'one will only see what one is ready to see; one will only learn what is on the edge of the consciousness of what one already knows' (Thomson 1984).

Whether teachers invite colleagues from in school or someone from outside (e.g. from a local higher education institution) will be a matter for their discretion. However, it may be worth noting that some research suggests that, 'It is preferable from the user's point of view to learn from a peer far enough from home so that: (1) asking for help can't be interpreted as a self-indictment; (2) invidious competition and comparison is reduced; (3) the ideas can be changed with impunity; (4) they can be credited to their new user' (Hopkins 1986). Whatever the choice, elements in *successful sharing* will be:

1 a willingness to share;
2 a recognition that sharing involves:
    (a) disclosure
    (b) opening oneself to the possibility of feedback;
3 a recognition that disclosure and feedback imply being prepared to consider changing;
4 Unless they become a regular part of the classroom over time, then children and teacher may react to their presence in such a way as to cause untypical behaviour;
5 a recognition that changing is sometimes:

(a) threatening (to self esteem and current practice)
(b) difficult (it requires time, energy, new skills)
(c) satisfying;
6 a recognition that the degree to which people are willing to share may, therefore, be restricted.

The results of this kind of interaction, if successful, will be more effective teaching standards. But the process will also generate documented information which may be used by teachers as part of an appraisal interview and as a means of helping the representatives of their employers (whether LEA advisers/inspectors or HMI) who might be visiting the school for the purpose of evaluation or inspection to gain an informed view and context for their own interpretations and judgements. Below is a summary of some of the advantages and disadvantages of the use of a critical friend which should be considered:

Advantages of critical friends (from inside or outside the school)

Providing they are skilled and trusted, they:

1 Can lighten the energy and time loads for observation (enable teacher to carry on teaching, maintain his or her duties).
2 Are likely to be less biased and more objective.
3 Can offer, where appropriate, comparisons with classroom practice elsewhere.
4 Can move freely and see the children working in different situations.
5 Can focus in on agreed issue or area of concern, e.g. small group task work.
6 Can provide post-lesson critical dialogues.
7 Can be used to check against bias in self-reporting, and to assist in more lengthy processes of self-evaluation.
8 In addition: children may be more open with outsiders (e.g. in interviews).

Disadvantages

If they are unskilled and not trusted then:

1 Unless a regular visitor their interpretations may be out of context.
2 Children may be less open with outsider (e.g. in interviews).
3 Observers will have their own biases.
4 Unless they become a regular part of the classroom over time, then children and teacher may react to their presence in such a way as to cause untypical behaviour.

In addition

5 The exercise is time consuming – observer and teacher must spend time together before and after the work observed to negotiate and fulfil the contract.
6 Observers are difficult to find!

Appraisal from below

Appraisal from below is already an implicit part of all teachers' working lives. It is possible, of course, for the teacher to ignore pupil feedback in the classroom or to be selectively inattentive for a short time; and it is possible for the headteacher to ignore staff feedback for a little longer. But to ignore the appraisals of 'subordinates' for any length of time is to place at risk your credibility to lead, whether it be in the classroom or staffroom. It follows, then, that 'appraisal from below' must form a part of any systematic appraisal scheme. Heads, as well as teachers, must find new ways of collecting information about themselves. One example of this is to:

1 create a list of skills and qualities which you think you should have;
2 rate yourself;
3 ask teachers and others (parents, children, governors) to rate you using the same list);
4 compare their perceptions with your own.

Ideally, all four of the appraisal systems described in this chapter – self-appraisal from above, peer appraisal, and appraisal from below – should combine. Not all will be carried out at the same time, nor for the same specific purposes, but all may contribute to a teacher profiling system which is in itself a part of a school's staff development policy.

No discussion of different systems of appraisal would be complete without at least a reference to the possibilities of linking teacher appraisal with pupil performance. While this will be anathema to all those who are only too well aware of the dangers of imposing a direct cause and effect relationship upon the complex business of teaching and learning, it is, nevertheless, a nettle which must be grasped.

Pupil outcomes and teacher performance

Everyone is concerned with maintaining and improving the quality of learning for pupils, and in many LEAs this concern has been documented in the form of 'Curriculum Guidelines'. These ensure that pupils receive certain key areas of experience. At national level also the Government has shown its concern by producing a series of 'Matters for Discussion' both across the curriculum (DES 1985) and in particular subject areas. Some of these have become policy, and more are likely to follow, so that in a short time it may be that there will be a national curriculum imposed on schools. It is a short step from this to appraising teachers on the basis of pupil performance in national tests which are to be related to key elements of this national curriculum. Some LEAs have already taken this step and begun, for example, to specify that, at the end of the infant stage of education most children should be able to:

- tell the time to within 5 minutes and use the calendar;
- understand that amounts of liquids or solids stay the same whatever the size and shape of their container;
- estimate and measure various utensils like cups, beakers and jam jars, and use rules and scales in both imperial and metric measure;
- recognise coins and use them to buy and sell, giving change;
- add, subtract and multiply numbers up to 20, and develop some idea of what simple division is, and work with numbers up to 100;

- arrange objects in groups according to size, shape or colour;
- know about common flat shapes like squares, triangles and circles and three dimensional shapes like cubes, spheres and cones.

(Croydon 1985)

The same document continues by outlining what pupils should have achieved by the age of eleven.

Regardless of whether the above 'objectives' are realistic or desirable for all children in all schools in one particular LEA or indeed for all children in all schools in every part of the country, the implications of this for the teacher are clear – that if pupils have not achieved these objectives reasons must be found, and it is likely that teachers will be held accountable. The logic of this is that there will be, at the very least, a temptation for teachers to teach to objectives which, like those above, are reasonably easy to assess through testing. However, Dean (1983) warns against giving 'too much importance to what can be measured and too little on the more complex kinds of learning which demonstrate understanding, particularly in a climate which stresses the need to be accountable'. She goes on to state also that, 'You can only assess what is evident. A child may know and be able to do much more than he can demonstrate in a test situation . . .'

Our hope is that pupil performance and teacher appraisal will not be linked. However, if it is, then it is important that 'performance' is not taken to mean the attainment of only behavioural objectives. The use of behavioural objectives represents an attempt to improve teaching effectiveness by matching learning outcomes with teaching intentions. This is a useful notion but it does have severe limitations if universally applied. Jackson summarises these when he writes that:

> The business of teaching involves much more than defining curricular objectives and moving towards them with despatch; and even that limited aspect of a teacher's work is far more complicated in reality than an abstract description of the process would have it seem. When it is remembered that the average teacher is in charge of the twenty-five or thirty students of varying abilities and backgrounds for approximately 1,000 hours a year and that his responsibilities extend over four or five major curriculum areas, it is difficult to see how he could be very precise about where he is going and how to get there during each instructional moment. He may have a vague notion of what he hopes to achieve, but it is unreasonable to expect him to sustain an alert awareness of how each of his students is progressing toward each of a dozen or so curricular objectives.

(Jackson 1968)

Behavioural objectives are not worthless. Indeed a systematic approach to planning and evaluating represents an advance on the purely intuitive. However, they do have deficiencies, and these have been comprehensively critiqued elsewhere (Macdonald-Ross 1973). It is as well to remember that there are other kinds of objectives which usually apply to higher order learning. These have been described as 'expressive' or 'problem solving' (Eisner 1979) and they take account of the individuality of the individual, and affective as well as cognitive achievements. Arguably the former are more important in education for living than the latter.

Ideally, of course, a balance is needed. However, an emphasis upon the use of behavioural objectives for assessment or appraisal purposes may mean that the complex, higher order areas of learning which teachers might wish to encourage but which are more difficult to test or quantify, will become less valued by them – particularly if pupil performance and teacher appraisal are directly linked.

The use of more regular and public appraisal in schools is likely to cause teachers to seek alternative strategies for self-evaluation and these will need to include the systematic collection and sharing of data from their classrooms, both for internal purposes of professional growth and external purposes of validation. The next chapter provides examples of approaches to and techniques for the collection of classroom data.

5 Inquiring into classroom action

The one undisputed requirement of good education is good teaching and performance in the classroom lies at the heart of the teacher's professional skill and of the standards of learning achieved, by helping to create the conditions in which effective learning and teaching can take place. It would be foolish to concentrate on any single aspect of teachers' performance without taking account of all the activities of the teaching day, and above all the context in which the teachers' professional tasks are performed.

(DES 1985)

If evaluation is to be taken seriously, then, it must occur 'at the business end in the classroom' (Shipman 1974). Indeed, the Graham Report (1985) suggests that 'It is important that classroom observation is seen to be central to the process' of appraisal. With all the variables that impinge upon or distort the ability to find a direct cause and effect relationship between teaching and learning, and since much higher order learning – as distinct from basic skill learning – is by its nature delayed, the use of classroom observation as a part of an appraisal process is, to say the least, problematic. There are issues of generalisability of findings (from one classroom and one school to another) because teaching intentions, conditions and pupil backgrounds differ. Equally important are issues concerning validity of information collected as well as finding appropriate methods of data collection. In addition there are questions concerning who collects the data, who owns it, who has the right to interpret and judge, and what are the criteria for judging what is a good lesson, what is a good teacher and what is effective pupil learning. While this part of the chapter will consider these issues, its primary function is rooted in the assumption that 'the ultimate test of any policy or initiative is whether it secures real improvement at the level where it really counts.... Improvement starts and ends with quality of pupil learning' (Taylor 1985).

It will, therefore, focus upon the means which teachers who are responsible in the classroom for the quality of pupil learning may use to monitor and evaluate their work. This distinction between monitoring and evaluation is important in the process of appraisal since 'Evaluation (or assessment) is the appraisal of the worth of something while monitoring is the collection of information which is relevant to making such an appraisal' (Elliott 1978).

The chapter therefore provides examples of a number of techniques for monitoring classrooms by self and others which are practical and which provide ideas for the design of action plans by teachers themselves.

The context of inquiry

Classroom observation is a necessity for those who wish to gain a greater understanding of what is happening. This implies that all teachers should have the opportunity at times in their teaching lives to engage in systematic data collection. Yet conditions of service for most teachers make this difficult to achieve. Traditionally, primary school teachers do not have the time to step outside the classroom to reflect. Most teachers' days are spent in isolation in the classroom working with children. While they will consciously reflect upon their practice, for some this will be irregular, for others regular, and for others a systematic occurrence. Few will systematically collect and analyse data as a part of the reflective process and incorporate the results of this into their practices. In addition, teachers will be at different stages of development as reflective practitioners and for a move from 'single-loop' to 'double-loop' learning to occur (see Chapter 2) which in itself increases the likelihood of sustained change, the support of the kind of consultant or critical friend described in the previous chapter may be needed.

Even in those schools which have enhanced staffing or the provision of supply days for the purpose of encouraging such kinds of professional development it is likely still that most of the data collection will occur *in situ* during the time when teaching and learning is occurring. Unless they are in a school with a 'non-teaching' head who is willing to arrange for cover, teachers have little opportunity for standing outside in order to reflect upon the action; to pursue systematic inquiries; or to visit classrooms of colleagues in their own or other schools in order to observe and, where appropriate, assist them in self-evaluation. The business of classroom inquiry is, therefore, constrained not only by factors of time and energy, but also, because formal self-evaluation has not traditionally been a part of a teacher's initial training, in many cases by a lack of knowledge of what may be available to assist in classroom inquiry.

Harlen (1977) has defined observation as being 'the process of gathering information during the course of day to day interaction between a teacher and her pupils'. She gives examples of the ways in which different kinds of observation can help teachers, 'become sensitive to children's thinking and feeling' i.e.

- dialogue with children (exchanging views (open ended) or questioning (directive));
- questioning (subject centred v. person centred);
- listening ('we may not hear all that the children have to say because we are talking' and 'we may not attend to the significance of what is said');
- watching actions and working processes (e.g. 'of children we *aren't* talking to');

- looking at the products.

Teachers observe classroom action as a natural part of their everyday professional lives. They need to do this in order to survive and to attempt to take into account the needs of the children and the needs of society as expressed through the school curriculum. At the end of the day they are, after all, held to be accountable for the progress in learning of each child in their care. When asked what they did to monitor pupil performance, one group of teachers listed the following:

1 observe constantly;
2 talk to children;
3 listen to children;
4 compare impressions with colleagues;
5 compare individuals with rest of group, class, age-range;
6 check daily, weekly, termly, annually;
7 use objective/published/standardised tests;
8 obtain feedback from parents;
9 produce profiles;
10 note children's responses.

(Roger and Richardson 1985)

All of these information-gathering exercises are essentially means which teachers use to identify what Zaltman *et al* (1977) suggest as a major force for change in education, 'the performance gap, or felt discrepancy between what is and what ought to be'. They suggest that the identification of 'performance gaps, developed through conditions internal or external to a system... stimulate a search for alternative actions that would better satisfy needs (i.e. lessen or close the gap). When such a search tends to an acceptable alternative course of action which is implemented, either by individuals or groups, change is said to have occurred'. Similarly, Argyris and Schon (1976) developed a theory of professional learning in which they suggest that each of us has a 'theory of action' which consists of two parts – our 'espoused theories' which are how we describe or explain teaching and our aspirations for teaching (our intentions) and our 'theories-in-use', which is our teaching behaviour (our practice). They suggest that in order to become more effective we must examine inconsistencies both within and between our intentions and practice.

Most teachers already have skills of *looking*, *listening* and *discussing* and these are used to elicit *feedback* on their teaching. However, although teachers are likely to be 'connoisseurs' (Eisner 1979) of teaching and learning, we have already seen (in Chapter 2) that much of this is at an intuitive, implicit level. In this sense teachers are 'theoryless'. Indeed, this may well be a positive advantage in terms of initiating and carrying out classroom inquiry. The frameworks suggested in this chapter attempt to take this practical problem into account. Indeed, they are rooted in the belief that:

> Reflection-in-action can occur in deliberate and calculated ways after the event, but it is just as likely to be an inseparable part of on-going practice. Where it occurs in the latter way, practitioners are in fact modifying their action in the

Table 5.1: Approaches to classroom inquiry (Adapted from Hook (1981) and Walker (1985))

Method	User	Advantages	Disadvantages	Examples of use
Anecdotal, records, field notes	Teacher, colleague or outsider	- aids recall - easy to operate - helps generate ideas - uncomplicated and cheap - cumulative records enable analysis for patterns, trends etc. - personal viewpoints - acts as an aide-memoire - used as a diary, enables for continuity and the building of a profile (by self or other) for use in appraisal as part of staff development	- selective - Impressionistic accounts which do not enable for checks against bias - do not allow direct recording of detailed data e.g. conversations - time consuming	- reflection on own teaching techniques as part of self appraisal - may be used as part of teacher profile - may be used as a first step towards more systematic action research - may be checked for bias by a trusted colleague invited into the classroom - may be used as a running commentary where the teacher or observer focus on an individual or small group and writes down as much of what she hears and observes as possible over a short period or 'critical incident' of, say, 5 minutes - may be used for 'pursuit' observation of an individual pupil over time
Interview	Teacher, colleague or outsider (e.g. parent)	- can be used during or outside teaching time (not disruptive) - enables direct access to	- time consuming - children may be unwilling or unable to reveal true opinions to outsider or	- obtain pupils or parents views on aspects of the curriculum - ideal when used with a tape stored and retrieved (but

| | | action
- can be used as one strand in triangulation (see p. 92)
- can be adjusted according to age of child, focus of inquiry
- can gain information while experience is fresh in pupils or teachers minds
- child may be at ease
- outsider can ask more objective questions | - colleague or outsider may be unfamiliar with pupils
- difficult to analyse interview data | confidentiality needs to be negotiated) |
|---|---|---|---|---|
| Questionnaire | Teacher, colleague or outsiders | - easily distributed
- provides confidential feedback | - design of questionnaire can be time consuming
- unsuitable for use with younger children
- may be irrelevant to teacher where questions have not been agreed by him/her
- analysis of responses can be time-consuming
- quantitative data collected can be simplistic and needs to be checked against qualitative data | - parents views of school policy
- teachers' views about resources, organisation etc.
- pupils views of school |

(continued)

Table 5.1 continued

Method	User	Advantages	Disadvantages	Examples of use
Observation schedules	Teacher, colleagues or outsiders	- quick method of recording - can occur during normal teaching hours - can be adapted for particular purposes - can be designed by teacher in collaboration with colleagues - can be used as a means of quantifying behaviour - can be used as a check against the possible bias of anecdotal records - special equipment not needed - if used by colleagues will be less subjective - if used by teachers, it may be time consuming to design - if used by teacher, it may have problems of objectivity	- may be difficult to use by the teacher (can interfere with teaching) - may need to occur over an extended period - if used on its own may distort and oversimplify classroom behaviour - if designed by outsiders may contain categories which are irrelevant to particular classroom situation - teacher and observer need to discuss schedule, its use and results. This may be time consuming. - skilled observers may be difficult to find	- analysis of teacher's questioning strategies - analysis of time spent by pupils in individual, small group class work - analysis of time spent by teacher with individual pupils
Audio recording	Teacher, colleagues, outsiders or pupils	- records all talk within range of equipment - portable cassette recorder can be easily	- transcription and analysis time consuming for teacher - pupils need to become	- analysis of teacher and pupil talk - recording interviews

		- carried by teacher during normal teaching
- recorder can be placed near individuals or small groups of pupils
- accurate means of collecting data to be retrieved and analysed later
- helps teacher focus
- use by colleagues or outsiders enables post lesson discussions to be based upon shared observable data	- used to its presence before they cease to become distracted or inhibited by it
- most recorders cannot adequately record groups of more than four or five
- extraneous noise may distort recording
- does not account for non-verbal communication which may influence interpretation
Photographs/ slides	Teacher, colleague, outsider or pupils	- provide a visual representation of the climate, organisation and teaching and learning strategies
- complement audio recording
- useful as accounts to share with others
- can provide a new perspective for the teacher	- cost may be prohibitive
- can be highly selective
- difficult for teacher to operate camera while teaching
- pupils may be distracted
- feedback will be delayed by processing time
- records nothing in depth
Video recordings	Teacher, colleagues outsiders or pupils	- combines sound and vision
- able to be reviewed either by self, self and colleagues, self and	- may be difficult to borrow equipment (but usually available) through teachers centre,	- record of classroom non-verbal climate, organisation, teaching and learning activities
- record of out of school field trips
- means of promoting discussion of school and classroom activities
- a means of sharing practice with colleagues and parents	- analysis of all teacher and pupil behaviour including talk, organisation, classroom movement

(continued)

Table 5.1 continued

Method	User	Advantages	Disadvantages	Examples of use
	outsider or self and pupils	- encourages self-confrontation - shows non-verbal behaviour - can be reviewed repeatedly enabling analysis and reanalysis - behavioural patterns may be identified - provides a comprehensive means of collecting and storage data for later use - patterns of progress over long periods can be charted	local comprehensive schools or IIE Institution by negotiation - more effectively used by colleague or outsider - can be intrusive and distracting to teacher and pupils (needs to be used over time so that it and the 'cameraman' become part of the furniture) - sound recording difficulties may arise - the camera can be selective	- a means of promoting self-confrontation of match or mismatch between teaching intentions and practices - a means of promoting discussion of shared observable classroom activities - a means of sharing practice with colleagues and parents

light of feelings and information about their own effects. They are not circumscribed by having to rely on knowledge generated by outside authorities; through monitoring what they do themselves, they have a way of knowing that is inherent in intelligent action.

(Smyth 1987)

Aids to classroom inquiry

It is, then, quite possible for most teachers to study their classrooms either on their own, or with the help of colleagues, parents, pupils or outside consultants. The instruments which may be used to help in this process of inquiry may range from anecdotal records and diaries, through checklists, observation schedules, interviews, questionnaires, still photographs, and audio and video recordings. Below is a summary of different techniques which may be used together with some of their advantages and disadvantages. The use of formal tests have not been included because it is assumed that these are widely used.

Getting started

In order to get started, teachers must decide on:

the WHY of observation. Decide what is the purpose. Is it primarily to solve a problem, or to check on the effectiveness of a particular strategy or aspect of curriculum content?

the WHAT of observation. This will be determined by either the teachers' own perceived interests, needs or concerns, or those of others.

the WHO of observation. Teachers should beware of being over-ambitious. For example, it may be sensible, if pupils are the focus, to observe one pupil or a small group; or if observing self it may be wise to focus on one aspect of teacher talk (e.g. questioning).

the WHEN of observation. Observation must be built in as a part of the teaching plan, and short concentrated periods of time for this *standing outside* actual contact with pupils may be more practical than long periods when the teacher is likely to be distracted.

the HOW of observation. Examples of techniques for collecting observations will be given later in the chapter. It is equally important, however, to find ways of organising the activity itself so that time and energy can be focused in support of the commitment; and frameworks for recording the information gained from classroom observations must also be devised.

One way of preparing the ground for any kind of classroom observation is to consider the whole chain of activities it serves. Figure 5.1 (p.88) may act as a kind of planning checklist for this data gathering technique.

The Open University's *Curriculum in Action: Practical Classroom Evaluation* (OU 1980) is one pack of materials offering practical guidance to teachers on how to carry out classroom evaluation. It focuses upon six questions about the curriculum

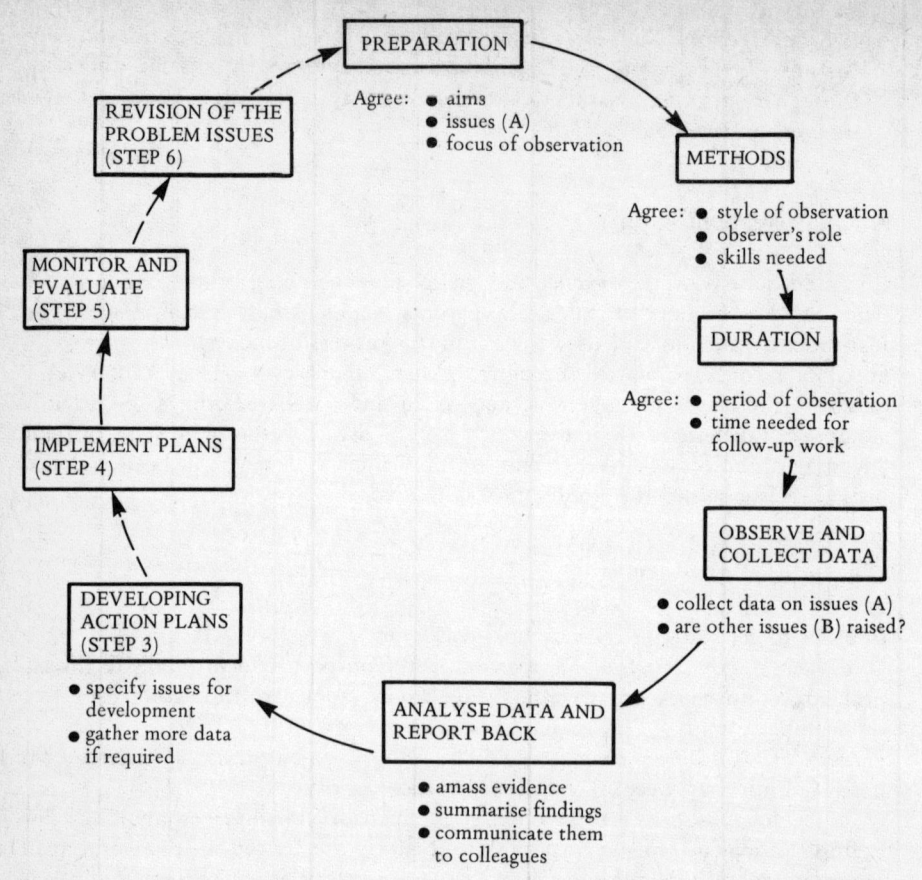

88 *Appraisal and professional development in the primary school*

```
                    PREPARATION
                         │
         Agree: • aims
                • issues (A)
                • focus of observation
                                    ↓
                                 METHODS
                         Agree: • style of observation
                                • observer's role
                                • skills needed
                                    ↓
                                 DURATION
                         Agree: • period of observation
                                • time needed for
                                  follow-up work
                                    ↓
                              OBSERVE AND
                              COLLECT DATA
                         • collect data on issues (A)
                         • are other issues (B) raised?

REVISION OF THE
PROBLEM ISSUES
(STEP 6)

MONITOR AND
EVALUATE
(STEP 5)

IMPLEMENT PLANS
(STEP 4)

DEVELOPING
ACTION PLANS
(STEP 3)
  • specify issues for
    development                ANALYSE DATA AND
  • gather more data           REPORT BACK
    if required
                               • amass evidence
                               • summarise findings
                               • communicate them
                                 to colleagues
```

Figure 5.1: Classroom observation: a sequence of activities (Farnsworth and Garcia 1985)

in action and provides detailed examples of ways of seeking answers to these. They are:

1 What did the pupils actually do?
2 What were they learning?
3 How worthwhile was it?
4 What did I do?
5 What did I learn?
6 What do I intend to do now?

These questions focus upon the three central elements in every classroom – the pupils (Questions 1 and 2), the task (Question 3) and the teacher (Questions 4, 5 and 6). Another way of representing the link between them is presented in Figure 5.2.

Notice that the link between teacher's intentions and practice is now explicit, and that the focus upon classroom action concerns the past, the present, and the future.

```
┌─────────────────────────┐
│ THE PUPILS              │
│ What did they actually do? │
│ What were they learing? │
└─────────────────────────┘
             │
             ▼
┌─────────────────────────┐        ┌──────────────────┐        ┌──────────────────┐
│ THE TASK                │───────▶│ What did I learn?│───────▶│ What do I        │
│ How worthwhile was it?  │        └──────────────────┘        │ intend to do     │
└─────────────────────────┘                                    │ now?             │
             ▲                                                 └──────────────────┘
             │
┌─────────────────────────┐
│ THE TEACHER             │
│ What did I do?          │
│ What did I intend to do?│
└─────────────────────────┘
```

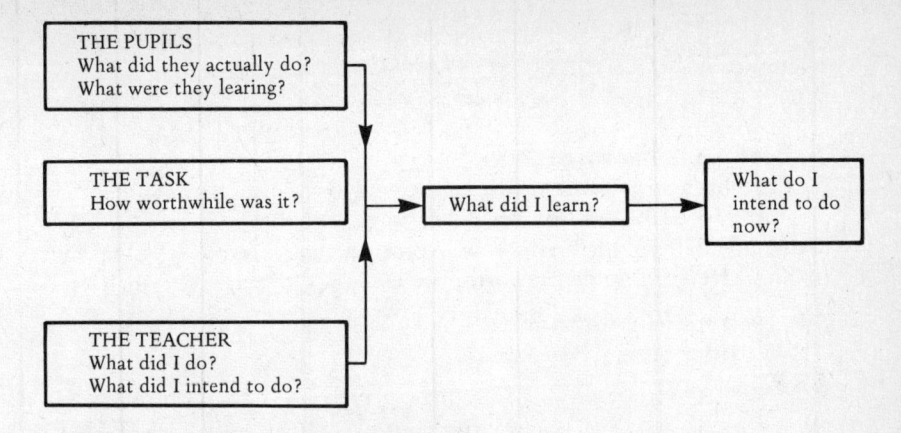

Figure 5.2: Focuses for classroom inquiry

Curriculum in Action provides valuable help in the systematic planning and analysis of aspects of classroom life. Below are examples of the advice given for planning focused observations and analyses of pupils:

1 Class discussion
(a) Make a plan for your classroom and during a discussion, or question and answer session, put ticks on your plan to show which children speak.
(b) Many possibilities for analysis will occur to you as you examine your findings. Here are some categories you could use to start your analysis:

- Pupils who were not involved in the session.
- Pupils who were involved on their own initiative.
- Pupils who were involved on my initiative.

(c) Notice any interesting or surprising patterns of behaviour: for example, has the seating plan any significance?
(d) Check the inferences you have made. What alternative interpretations/inferences could you make?
(e) What further questions have been raised for you?

2 Group work
(a) Choose a small group of pupils and observe how they work together.
(b) Many possibilities for analysis will occur to you as you examine your findings. Here are some categories you could use to start your analysis:

- Children working together to solve problems.
- Children working on their own for most of the time.
- Children disrupting the work of the group.

(c) Notice any interesting or surprising patterns of behaviour: for example, when do children seek help from others, when do some children disrupt the work of the group?

(d) Check the inferences you have made. What alternative interpretations/inferences could you make?
(e) What further questions have been raised for you?

3 Aspects of pupils' language
(a) Record what your pupils say to each other and to you on occasions other than when they are involved in class discussions.
(b) Many possibilities for analysis will occur to you as you examine your findings. Here are some categories you could use to start your analysis:

* Request for help with work.
* Request for general reassurance.
* Request for materials.

(c) Notice any interesting or surprising patterns of behaviour: for example, does any type of questioning predominate? How much talk is about work?
(d) Check the inference you have made. What alternative interpretations/inferences could you make?
(e) What further questions have been raised for you?

4 The quiet 'working' classroom
(a) Choose a time when your pupils appear to be working quietly at a task you have set them.

Try to find out from at least some of your pupils what they think this task entails. This may be seen as approaching the area of concern of Unit 3, but remember, you are still finding out what your pupils are doing, not what they are learning.

For example, a child asked to describe what he is doing as he colours a map might say: 'I'm doing this bit brown and this bit blue'. You will then need to question him further to find out if he really knows what these colours signify with refernce to the key which indicates that high areas are brown and the sea blue.

(Open University 1980)

Clearly, it is important to move systematically through a number of steps which involve:

Step 1: Choosing the investigation.
Step 2: Asking 'What learning opportunities am I trying to provide?'
Step 3: Deciding on the questions you want to ask.
Step 4: Designing the investigation
    (a) What data do I need to collect?
    (b) What should be the timing and circumstances of the investigation?
    (c) What techniques should I use?
Step 5: Carrying out the investigation.
Step 6: Analysing the data.
Step 7: Reflecting on the analysis.

Investigating an aspect of teaching (Open University 1980)

Classroom data will be used for a number of purposes as illustrated below:

Figure 5.3: The use of classroom data

- to identify match or mismatch between intentions and practices.
- to provide the basis for forming hypotheses for increasing professional effectiveness.
- to provide the basis for more focused observations into specific aspects of teaching and learning.
- to provide information to explain or justify classroom events to self and others e.g. in appraisal interviews.
- to help others (e.g. external observers) to understand the conditions of and interactions in the classroom.

For these purposes alone it will be necessary to check on the *validity* of interpretations and judgements that have been made of classroom life.

Below is an example of how to check where an inference or interpretation is soundly based on evidence, or unsubstantiated.

Figure 5.4: Checking whether an inference is soundly based on evidence, or unsubstantiated (Open University 1980)

Stage	*Example*
Observation	The teacher sees Darren talking to his neighbour.
Making an inference	The teacher records: 'Darren was wasting time.'
Checking the inference	The teacher ask: 'How do I know that Darren was wasting time?' The teacher remembers making this inference because Darren was talking to his neighbour.
Checking the quality of the evidence	The teacher asks: 'Is my evidence good enough?' The teacher realises that it is not sufficient. Darren was too far away at the time and could not be overheard.
Recognising the unsubstantiated inferences	The teacher says, 'Perhaps I was wrong to infer that Darren was wasting time' and goes on to ask: 'Then why did I make that inference?' The teacher realises that an expectation that Darren will waste time whenever possible has led to this kind of inference being made time and time again.
Making alternative interpretations or inferences	On the basis of the evidence available the teacher asks: 'Rather than wasting time could Darren have been asking for some help with his work? Could Darren have been responding to a request for help? Could Darren have been discussing the work in hand or could Darren have been chatting about last night's television or tomorrow's football match, and therefore wasting time after all?

One effective means of validating accounts of classroom action with the help of a colleague is available by means of *triangulation*. This process involves taking into account a number of views of the same event:

```
           The Teacher
             /\
            /  \
           /    \
          /      \
The Pupils ←————→ The Observer
```

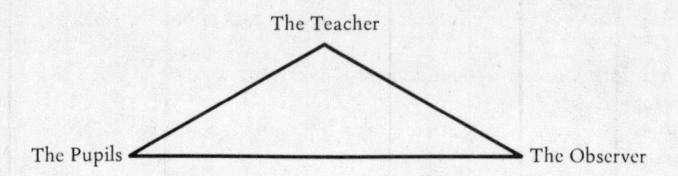

Figure 5.5: Triangulation as a means of validating interpretations of classrooms (Farnsworth and Garcia 1985)

Triangulation, then, involves gathering accounts of the teaching situation from three quite different points of view:

> Each point of the triangle stands in a unique epistemological position with respect to access to relevant data about a teaching situation. The teacher is in the best position, via introspection, to gain access to his own intentions and aims in the situation. The students are in the best position to explain how the teacher's actions influence the way they respond to the situation.
>
> (Farnsworth and Garcia 1985)

There are four clear implications for all those engaged in appraisal which arise from the acceptance of triangulation as a means of establishing validity of interpretation:

1 No single view of the classroom is necessarily the 'right' one. (No one has a monopoly on truth).
2 Interpretations of teaching and learning must be based upon negotiated and agreed criteria between appraisee and appraisor.
3 Pupils may have a more significant role to play in appraisal and self-evaluation than has been previously accepted.
4 Inferences from any one observation can be drawn only in relation to the context and the set of circumstances which operate on that particular occasion. Without a series of observations, generalisations are impossible to make. Appraisal is therefore temporary rather than permanent.

The next section provides examples of frameworks which can be used for observing classrooms explicitly and systematically. There is no expectation that any one of these will necessarily provide an ideal model for any teacher or group of teachers, but it is hoped that the examples may be adapted or used as springboards for the design of models appropriate to particular circumstances. Since it is recognised that sometimes teachers will want to gain a general view and at other times a more focused view of their classrooms examples of both are provided. Observations will have different purposes, e.g. to find out why a particular pupil is

Inquiring into classroom action 93

behaving in a particular way, to discover more about how children learn in groups, to trace the movements of a child between different activities, or to find out about the kinds of questions which the teacher uses when talking with individuals, groups or the whole class. However, there will inevitably be some gaps between intentions and practice. The logic of planning for teaching and the teaching itself will be different since the latter will be affected by the teacher-pupil interaction. The models can, of course, be used by peers and others as part of the appraisal process.

Frameworks for general classroom inquiry

The anecdotal report, based as it is on an impressionistic view of classroom events, is likely to be the most common form of self or peer appraisal used by teachers. This kind of reporting, relying as it does on the 'connoisseurship' of teachers, is one stage further along the road to systematic review than the undocumented reflection which is part of most teachers' intuitive learning equipment. The act of writing down views of classroom events in itself provides an important initial step in guarding against possible bias and distortion. It is important to remember that it is 'truth' rather than 'proof' which is the object of the exercise. No reporting can ever be entirely objective.

Whether the report is written after the event or whether it is based upon field notes collected during the event it is important to ensure that the teacher moves through five distinct sequential phases:

Figure 5.6: Five phases of reporting

1 Description of *what* is happening in the classroom.
2 Interpretation – assessing the consequences of what is happening.
3 Checking for bias in interpretative/inference.
4 Judgement – assessing for the worthwhileness of what has been observed against teachers' intentions and standards (criteria).
5 Decision – accepting responsibility for 1-3 and planning for future action.

The importance of beginning with description cannot be overemphasised since it ensures that any bias in interpretation, judgments and decisions can be checked against available observed action rather than assumptions or expectations or memories which a teacher might have about the action.

Making notes can act both as a means for further reflection and the generation of hypotheses. The notes may be shared with those made by an observer of the lesson and used as a basis for discussion and further planning. At the very least they can provide a vehicle for further thought. Where notes are made sequentially, in the form of a diary, for example, they enable reflection upon both sequence of events and emphases which are placed on particular learning organisation, activities and individual pupils.

Gronlund (1976) makes the following, very practical suggestions for teachers who wish to use anecdote as a means of recording observational assessment of pupils:

1. Determine in advance what to observe, but be alert for unusual behavior. We are more apt to select and record meaningful incidents if we review objectives and outcomes and decide which behaviours require evaluation by direct observation – that is, those which cannot be effectively evaluated by other means. We can further focus our observations by looking for just a few specific types of behaviour at any given time. While such directed observations are highly desirable for obtaining evidence of pupil learning there is always the danger that unique incidents which have special value for understanding a pupil's development will be overlooked. Consequently, we must be sufficiently flexible to note and report any unusual behavior in the event that it may be significant.
2. Observe and record enough of the situation to make the behaviour meaningful. It is difficult to interpret behavior apart from the situation in which it occurred. An aggressive action, such as pushing another child for example, might reflect good-natured fun, an attempt to get attention, a response to direct provocation, or a sign of extreme hostility. Clues to the meaning of behavior frequently can be obtained by directing attention to the actions of the other pupils involved and the particular setting in which the behavior took place. The record, therefore, should contain those situational conditions which seem necessary for understanding the pupil's behavior.
3. Make a record of the incident as soon after the observation as possible. In most cases it is infeasible to write a description of an incident at the time it happens. However, the longer we delay in recording observations, the greater the likelihood that important details will be forgotten. Making a few brief notes at opportune times following behavioral incidents and completing the records after school generally provides a feasible and satisfactory procedure.
4. Limit each anecdote to a brief description of a single specific incident. Brief and concise descriptions take less time to write, less time to read and are more easily summarized. Just enough detail should be included to make the description meaningful and accurate. Limiting each description to a single specific incident also simplifies the task of writing, using, and interpreting the records.
5. Keep the factual description of the incident and your interpretation of it separate. The description of an incident should be as accurate and objective as you can make it. This means stating exactly what happened in clear and nonjudgmental words. Avoid such terms as 'lazy, unhappy, shy, hostile, sad, ambitious, persistent', and the like. If used at all, reserve such words for the separate section in which you give your tentative interpretations of the incident. There is no need to interpret each incident, but when interpretations are given they should be kept separate and clearly labelled as such.
6. Record both positive and negative behavioral incidents. There is a general tendency for teachers to note more readily those behaviors which disturb them personally and which interfere with the on-going process in the

classroom. The result is that anecdotal records frequently contain a disproportionate number of incidents which indicate the lack of learning or development. For evaluation purposes, it is equally important to record the less dramatic incidents which provide clues concerning the growth that is taking place. Thus, a conscious effort should be made to observe and record these often more subtle positive behaviors as well as the more obvious negative reactions.

7 Collect a number of anecdotes on a pupil before drawing inferences concerning typical behavior. A single behavioral incident is seldom very meaningful in understanding a pupil's behavior. We all have our moments of 'peak performance' and 'extreme error proneness,' elation and despair, confidence and self-doubt. It is only after observing a pupil a number of times in a variety of settings that his basic pattern of behavior begins to emerge. Consequently, we should generally delay making any judgments concerning his learning or development until we have a sufficient sample of behavior to provide a reliable picture of how the pupil typically behaves in different situations.

8 Obtain practice in writing anecdotal records. At first, most teachers have considerable difficulty in selecting significant incidents, in observing them accurately, and in describing them objectively. Some training and practice is therefore desirable before embarking on the use of anedotal records. If the entire school staff is involved, a regular in-service training program should be provided. Where an individual teacher wants to explore their use in his own classroom, the aid of a supervisor or fellow teacher can be helpful in appraising the quality of the records. It might be wise to start by observing pupils' study habits during a study period, as this will provide sufficient time to observe and record significant behavior.

(Gronlund 1976)

An evaluation framework which takes account of both the planning of teaching and teaching itself has been designed by Robert Stake (1961). He divided planning and teaching into three segments.

1 Antecedents – conditions which exist prior to teaching taking place, e.g. pupils' abilities, school and classroom contexts, resources, teaching organisation, etc.
2 Transactions – what happens between pupils and between teacher and pupils during the lesson.
3 Outcomes – what pupils learn (including unintended or unplanned for learning).

He draws attention to the logical relationship between these three segments in the mind of the teacher who is planning for teaching and the 'here-and-now', empirical relationship between the segments which occurs in the 'delivery' of the teaching. He asserts that the two sets of relationships may be different, and suggests that if teachers are to increase their effectiveness, then they must seek to draw the two more closely together in order to achieve congruence.

This kind of framework, shown in Figure 5.7, can be useful in helping individual teachers to collect data about their classrooms. They may set out their

96 *Appraisal and professional development in the primary school*

Figure 5.7: A representation of the processing of descriptive data (Stake 1969)

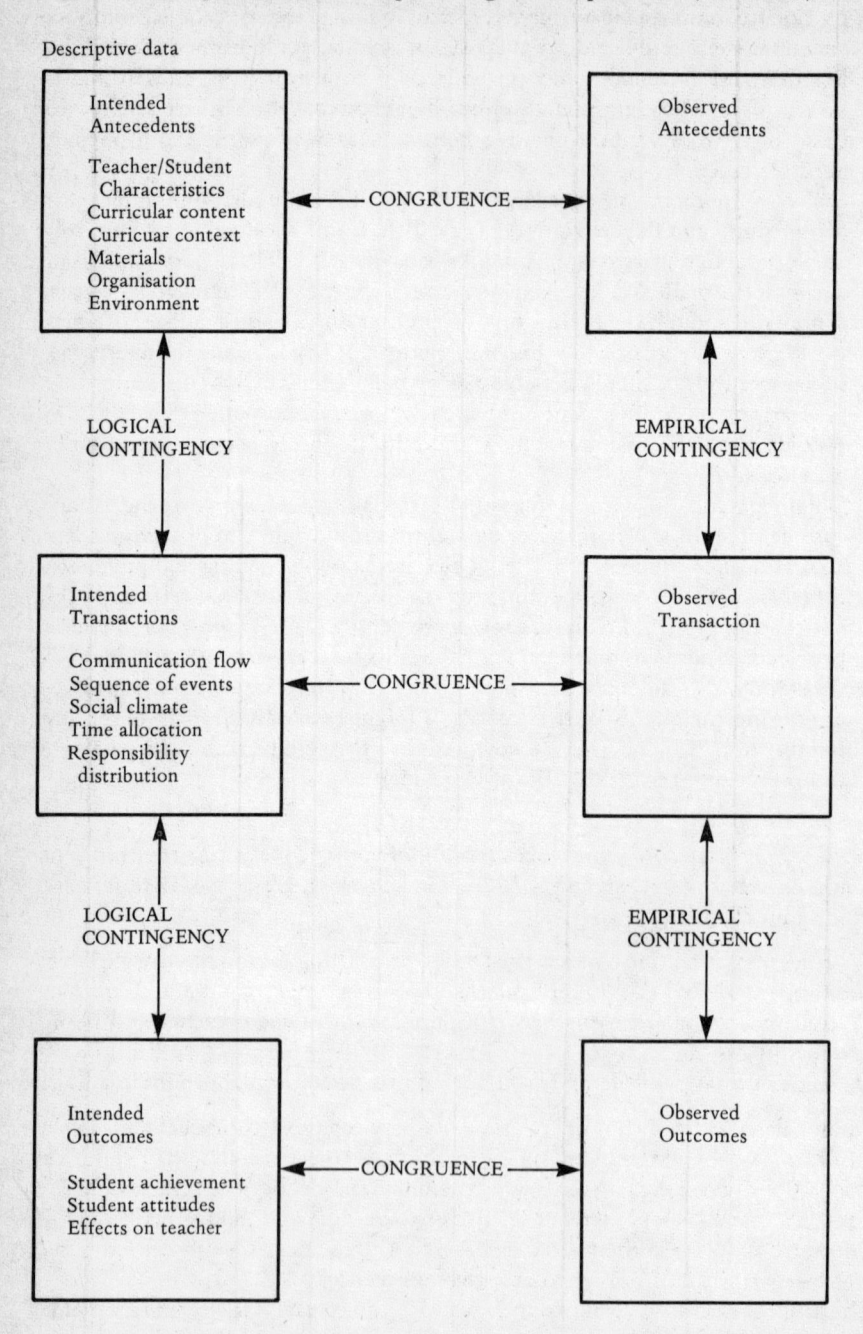

Descriptive data

```
┌─────────────────────┐                           ┌─────────────────────┐
│ Intended            │                           │ Observed            │
│ Antecedents         │                           │ Antecedents         │
│                     │                           │                     │
│ Teacher/Student     │                           │                     │
│  Characteristics    │◄──── CONGRUENCE ────►     │                     │
│ Curricular content  │                           │                     │
│ Curricuar context   │                           │                     │
│ Materials           │                           │                     │
│ Organisation        │                           │                     │
│ Environment         │                           │                     │
└─────────▲───────────┘                           └─────────▲───────────┘
          │                                                 │
     LOGICAL                                           EMPIRICAL
     CONTINGENCY                                       CONTINGENCY
          │                                                 │
┌─────────▼───────────┐                           ┌─────────▼───────────┐
│ Intended            │                           │ Observed            │
│ Transactions        │                           │ Transaction         │
│                     │                           │                     │
│ Communication flow  │                           │                     │
│ Sequence of events  │◄──── CONGRUENCE ────►     │                     │
│ Social climate      │                           │                     │
│ Time allocation     │                           │                     │
│ Responsibility      │                           │                     │
│  distribution       │                           │                     │
└─────────▲───────────┘                           └─────────▲───────────┘
          │                                                 │
     LOGICAL                                           EMPIRICAL
     CONTINGENCY                                       CONTINGENCY
          │                                                 │
┌─────────▼───────────┐                           ┌─────────▼───────────┐
│ Intended            │                           │ Observed            │
│ Outcomes            │                           │ Outcomes            │
│                     │                           │                     │
│ Student achievement │                           │                     │
│ Student attitudes   │◄──── CONGRUENCE ────►     │                     │
│ Effects on teacher  │                           │                     │
└─────────────────────┘                           └─────────────────────┘
```

plans for their work in the left hand sections and complete the right hand sections retrospectively and separately and, as far as possible, without comparing the two initially. Once this has been done, they can reflect upon the relationship between the two segments. Where colleagues are used as observers they will be able to have foresight of the teacher's intentions. Knowledge of these is essential if observers and teachers are to establish a dialogue about teaching which arises from mutual understanding without which trust cannot be built.

The lesson profile below provides another simple framework for use in structuring an impressionistic observation of the way in which teachers organise different tasks and the time allocated.

Table 5.2: Lesson profile (Walker and Adelman 1975)

	Time			
	10 mins	20 mins	30 mins	10 mins
Teacher Activity	Settling in; Giving out books	Introduces experiment; Gives directions; Asks questions	Moves round helping small groups working on experiments	Clearing up
Pupil	Finishing work from last lesson	Listening to teacher's directions; Answering questions	Working on experiments	Write up results of
Resources	Text books; pens; exercise books		Bunsen burners; tongs; foodstuffs; balances	Exercise books, pens

This provides evidence of the way a teacher allocates time to particular activities or tasks and what he or she and the pupils do. In this way it aids reflection upon relative time allocation (of activities) and roles (of teacher and pupils) generally. However, the word 'task' concerns both the process and the product of working. Since a concern for the pupils' tasks will be at the heart of every teacher's work and their behaviour in the classroom, it will be likely that, from time to time, teachers will wish to examine in more detail the relationship between their control over the tasks and the pupils' learning.

There appears to be a relationship, then, between the structure of task activities and degree of control necessary to perform that activity: the amount of teacher dominance over classroom events may be related, in part, to the characteristics of instructional tasks.

(Bossert 1977)

Teacher-pupil roles and task organisation

The way teachers plan their curriculum and the way this planning is expressed in their acts give a clear indication to pupils of the teacher's intentions and thus the position that they wish them to occupy in the learning which they must undertake. Do they, for example, wish them to passively assimilate knowledge which only they possess? Or do they wish them to participate by encouraging them to make their own meanings; and to influence the content, process and product of their own work. Do they consult them about what they do and how they should do it? This will, of course, depend upon teaching intentions, and, as we know:

> Good teachers need a variety of approaches and patterns of working, and the flexibility to call on several different strategies within the space of one lesson. Sound planning and skilful management are needed to blend class, group and individual work, to provide a wide range of learning activities, to observe, to solve problems, to offer explanations and to apply skills and ideas.
>
> (DES 1985)

However, we also know that recently available evidence (as distinct from aspiration or intention) of teaching in junior schools shows:

> that a vast majority of junior school teachers are firmly in control of their classrooms. They determine what activities their pupils will undertake; they prefer a didactic approach rather than a reliance on discovery methods; they are making increased use of class teaching; and there is no need to exhort them to go back to the basics. Indeed the development of and practice in the basic skills both of English and of mathematics would seem to be the predominant features of junior school classrooms...
>
> (Barker-Lynn 1984)

It may well be useful, then, for teachers who subscribe to the child-centred, progressive education which was the hallmark of the Plowden Report (1967) to check up on their practice by focusing upon teaching organisation, pupils' roles, and teacher-pupil relationships as expressed through classroom talk. (See Table 5.3).

This checklist, like the lesson profile before it, will present evidence of a focused but general nature, and it may well be that teachers would wish to observe an individual or group of pupils, or, as we have suggested, analyse the kinds of talk which he or she is using.

Table 5.3: Teaching organisation, pupil roles, and teacher-pupil relationships

Lesson Content	Comments

Teaching Organisation

Points to consider

1 Are the pupil tasks imposed/negotiated? To what extent?
2 What is the organisation of the teaching group(s) within the classroom?
3 Is the emphasis on content coverage of teacher-selected material?

Pupils' Roles

Points to consider

1 Are they expected to
   (a) assimilate the teacher's knowledge,
   (b) find 'correct' answers to teachers questions,
   (c) present opinions, facts, hypotheses,
   (d) initiate conversations,
   (e) exercise degrees of control over the content, direction and pacing of the tasks?

Classroom Talk

Points to consider

1 What is the nature/quality of teacher-pupil talk?
2 Who initiates talk?
3 How much participation by pupils is there in the talk?
4 How long does the teacher talk and how long does the pupil talk?

Pupil pursuit

One example of a systematic series of observations of individual pupils has been documented by a First School teacher (Haydon, 1986). Over a period of time, she observed pupils' task behaviour and devised and developed a series of checklists which helped her in the process. From simple observations she drew up a grid with working notes:

Observation Number 7
Name: Neil (8 years)   *Date*: 25 June
Time started: 9.25   *Finished*: 9.55   *Interval*: 1 min

Table 5.4: Pupil pursuit (Haydon 1986)

minutes	1	2	3	4	5	6	7	8	9	10	11	12	13	14	15	16	17	18	19	20	21	22	23	24	25	26	27	28	29	30
On Task Working by self			x						x	x				x	x	x	x	x	x						x				x	
On Task Working & talking																												x		x
On Task Talking about work				x																		x								
Off Task Talking	x				x	x	x																							
Off Task Walking																			x		x									
Off Task Disruptive																				x			x	x	x	x				
Teacher Interaction			x									x														x				
Solitary - off task																														

Lesson: Maths/English - know which work to do.
Notes two boys sitting back to window but away from rest the of the class
(Neil/Michael)

Number Extra Notes
1   Drawing £ sign on desk to →Michael (M)
2   t → (M)
3   Reading Maths book - to (T) 4
5   Discussing Maths → (M)
6   David collecting some finished work - t → (D)
7   t → (M) + 8
9/10   Working - no talking!!
12   (T) to whole class 'It's about time you all settled down and got some work done!'
20   Putting maths book away - crossing room - looking at others as he went.
21   Back at desk - searching - disrupting (M)
22   Back across room looking for English book - t → (M)
23   Opening book - find place to work - t → (M)
24   As 1 writing pencil on table top - doodle?
27   Getting dictionary for work - caused disruption to another table - on return from getting dictionary.
        tT = teacher

Here are the comments she made and the questions which were raised as a result of her investigation.

Comments

Neil produced a seven minute span of concentration when he was working by himself totally engrossed - this was probably caused by my intervention at 12 - when I told all the class to 'settle down'. He had been talking about his work to Michael prior to this and I noticed that when Michael was unable to answer his questions he came and asked me - unfortunately he didn't then return and continue working. Nearly all his talk was with Michael as they were sitting together and away from the others. When David went to collect some work for me (which was still in Neil's desk) it led to a chat before David could return - Neil also talked to some other children when he went to put his book away. There was a period of about ten minutes before he was able to settle down again with his English after finishing his Maths - partly because it took him a while to find his English book (his desk is not very tidy and even less so after looking for his book!!).

I didn't like seeing him drawing on the top of his desk, saw him doing it twice, must have words next time. At 27 recorded him walking and being disruptive - he managed at this point to stop a whole table from working as he went past.

Questions raised by the observation
1 How much time do we spend with each child? I notice only two checkmarks for teacher interaction, 4. He came to me and 12. I spoke to whole class.

2 How long is it reasonable to expect anyone to be 'on-task?'
3 How does their interest in the task, or lack of it, affect the time they are prepared to concentrate?

What do I intend to do now?
Try some observations on other children using the same format.

From this she developed a further observation schedule and notes.

Observation Number 8
Aim to find out how much time in a given lesson a child is engaged 'on-task' (working as you expect on a given task) or 'off-task' (talking not connected with the task, sharpening pencil, etc.)

minutes	1	2	3	4	5	6	7	8	9	10	11	12	13	14	15	16	17	18	19	20	21	22	23	24	25	26	27	28	29	30	31
On-task																															
Off-task																															

Expected On-task Responses	Expected Off-task Responses

Number	Extra Notes

Notes
1 Used in its most simple form this observation requires a tick every one or two minutes to record if the child is 'on-task' or 'off-task'.
2 Each observation is numbered so that with the use of a digital watch the number can be related to the minutes: no. 1 at 10.21; no. 2 at 10.22, etc – if you miss one or two just leave a gap.

3 For all uses of this observation decided on child and enter details of lesson and time interval to be used.
4 Then try one of the following ways:
   (a) as 1 above
   (b) Using the note space jot down any outside influences which may cause an 'off-task' response (window-cleaner, visitor to room, another child being disruptive) – you can use the observation number to record this, e.g. 8/9/10 went to toilet
   14 talking to John
   any 'on-task' responses that you wish to record may be noted in the same way.
   (c) Based on your knowledge of this child you will have some ideas or assumptions about various 'on/off-task' activities that you could expect to see. It makes an interesting development to write these down first and then see if you find any evidence.

It may be that you will find no evidence for your assumptions. As one teacher found out having described a boy as 'quiet, hardly knew he was there', then after completing this type of observation said that the child had 'never stopped talking'. The observation had disclosed that his talking had been quiet and therefore not disruptive to the rest of the class, the reason for the teacher's assumption was that the boy didn't talk much to the teacher.

(Haydon 1986)

Teacher-pupil interaction

Talk

Jackson (1968) pointed out that children spend more than a thousand hours in school each year. For much of this time they will be listening to their teacher and learning not only from the content of what he or she says but also from the kinds of talk which are used. For example, talk will be a principle means of maintaining social control in the classroom as well as communicating knowledge. The pupils will also learn, from the form of the teacher's statements and questions, what constitutes valid knowledge and what part they are to play in the shaping of knowledge. Are they, for example, to be passive receivers or active makers of knowledge? Clearly, teachers will want pupils to be both 'receivers' and 'makers' at different times, but it will be useful, from time to time, to check that the form of language which they use is appropriate to their intentions. Douglas Barnes (1976), for example, distinguished four categories of teacher questioning:

Factual (what?) questions which demand information
Reasoning (how? or why?) questions which demand observation, recall or more open-ended reasoning
Open questions, not demanding reasoning
Social questions, intended either to control the class or seeking them to share experience

Finally, he identified *Pseudo* questions in which the teacher appears to be asking for personal views, opinions, or reasons but really has a particular answer in mind (Stubbs 1976). Here is how one teacher defined his interest in seeking to analyse his questioning in the classroom:

> OPEN AND CLOSED QUESTIONS
>
> In order to achieve my aims with the children and to keep a dialogue going between pupils and myself, I ask as many questions as possible. I aim to ask *open* questions as frequently as possible, as they will be more likely to invite a response from the children other than a simple 'yes' or 'no' to the question posed. By definition, therefore, open questions are those which invite some response from the children other than a straight 'yes' or 'no' or just a one word answer. In most cases there is not necessarily one answer only, but any number of alternative answers which could be accepted by me, by the children... Also by definition *closed* questions are the opposite of open ones, asking for a straightforward 'yes' or 'no' from the children, or else where there is only one correct response possible as an answer to a question.'
>
> (Open University 1981)

This teacher made audio-recordings of his work, and made a written transcript of this. He was then able to reflect upon and analyse the types of questions he used *in relation to his intentions*.

Below is a schedule developed for infant teachers by Bassey and Hatch (1979). Again, audio-recording is used, but this time the replay can be coded against seven categories of classroom talk and applied to individual children.

Figure 5.8: Infant teacher classroom speech schedule

Q Teacher asks a question
D Teacher gives a direction
I Teacher gives some information
E Teacher gives encouragement
C Teacher checks undesirable behaviour or performance
P Teacher gives, or declines to give, permission for a child to do something
X Teacher says something which is not classifiable under any of the above headings.

Figure 5.9: An example of instant coding of 3 minutes of teacher talk

D	/E	/E	/E (QD)	D/Q	/P/QQD	
Tim	Simon	Kirsty	Tina	Juhara	Michael	Deborah
Down	Simon	Katie	Class	Kirsty		

(Coded by Teacher A: 26 utterances; 13 interactions

In itself, this means little, but in relation to the teacher's intentions for each child, and with the benefit of additional codings, it may be possible for the teacher to build up a profile of her treatment of individual pupils.

Pupils talking: exploratory and final draft talk

Douglas Barnes (1976) distinguished between two kinds of talk in which children engaged in different settings. He found that many teachers demanded 'final draft' talk from pupils. In this, on-the-spot answers to questions, contributions to discussion were demanded which did not allow time for thought, reflection or negotiation of meanings by pupils, either with each other or with teacher. He postulated a relationship between (1) the teacher's view of knowledge, (2) what the teacher values in the pupils, (3) the teacher's view of his or her own role and (4) the teacher's evaluation of the pupil's participation. Consequently, he differentiated between two 'ideal types' of teacher – the 'transmission' and 'interpretation'. These two 'types' relate to the 'expository' and 'hypothetical' modes of classroom talk which had been suggested by Bruner (1961).

In *Expository* talk, 'decisions concerning the mode and pace of style of exposition are principally determined by the teacher as expositor; the student is the listener. The speaker has quite a different set of decisions to make: (s)he has a wide choice of alternatives; (s)he is anticipating paragraph content while the listener is still intent upon the words; (s)he is manipulating the content of the material by various transformations while the listener is quite unaware of these internal options'.

In *Hypothetical* talk, 'teacher and student are in a more co-operative position with respect to what in linguistics would be called "speakers' decisions". The student is not a bench bound listener, but is taking part in the formulation and at times may play the principal role in it. (S)he will be aware of alternatives and may even have an "as if" attitude towards these, and he may evaluate information as it comes' (Bruner 1961).

While there is no suggestion that any one teacher will necessary fit into only one of the categories they do provide a useful reference point for reflection upon the general nature of classroom communication.

GROUP WORK

Barnes further speculated that, while there should be both kinds of talk – exploratory and final draft – in classrooms, the former was more likely to occur in 'intimate' small group settings, though even here there would be variables:

Figure 5.10: Classroom talk audiences (Barnes 1976)

Variable	Intimate	Distant
Size	Small group	Full class or large group
Source of authority	The group	The teacher
Social relationships	Intimate	Public
Ordering of thought	Inexplicit	Explicit
Speech	Hesitant	Pre-planned
Functions	Exploratory	Final draft

It is worthwhile, in organising groupwork in class, to pose the question of its function, and in relation to this, teacher and pupil roles.

TEACHER LED DISCUSSIONS

Finally in this section on teacher-pupil talk it may be worth observing the relative degree of teacher-pupil dominance or control over both the selection of knowledge and the processes of learning. Below are some hypotheses derived from the Ford Project in which groups of teachers who were interested in pursuing an inquiry mode of teaching joined with researchers to define 'inquiry' and to find out whether their practice and intentions matched (Elliott and Adelman 1976).

> Panel 4.4 Some hypotheses about teacher-led discussions (after Adelman, Elliott et al)
>
> 1 Asking many questions of pupils ... may raise too many of the teacher's own ideas and leave no room for those of the pupils. Responding to pupils' questions with many ideas may stifle the expression of their own ideas.
> 2 Re-formulating problems in the teacher's own words may prevent pupils from clarifying them for themselves.
> 3 When the teacher changes the direction of enquiry or point of discussion, pupils may fail to contribute their own ideas. They will interpret such actions as attempts to get them to comform with his own line of reasoning.
> 4 When the teacher always asks a question following a pupil's response to his previous question, he may prevent pupils from introducing their own ideas.
> 5 When the teacher responds to pupils' ideas with utterances like 'good', 'yes', 'right', 'interesting', etc., he may prevent others from expressing alternative ideas. Such utterances may be interpreted as rewards for providing the responses required by the teacher.
>
> (Sutton 1981)

PUPIL 'WAIT-TIME'

Another way of thinking about pupil participation in thinking and talking in class is to assess the interrelationship between teacher and pupil action in terms of 'wait-time'. John Hayson (1985) reports on the work of Mary Budd Rowe. She:

> ... had become aware of the way many teachers were seemingly content to accept short responses from their pupils when they were answering questions. She was also aware that people in general frequently pause for thought when they are talking. What would happen, she speculated, if teachers introduced 'wait-time' after a question and after a pupil responds?
>
> Her findings were dramatic. Not only did the length of pupils' responses increase but failure to respond decreased. The pupils seemed to grow in confidence – fewer responses were inflected, the number of unsolicited but appropriate responses increased, and the contributions by 'slow' children increased as well. The incidence of speculative thinking grew and more pupil-pupil communication took place. And, moreover, the changed patterns of response seemed to affect the teacher, teacher-centred show-and-tell decreased...

UNDERSTANDING V JUDGING
In terms of the teacher's role as assessor it might be useful to analyse teacher-pupil conversations by devising a checklist based on Figure 5.11 below.

Figure 5.11: Understanding versus judging (Barnes 1976)

UNDERSTANDING——————VERSUS——————JUDGING

UNDERSTANDING	JUDGING
Accepts idea	Positive evaluation ('good')
Clarifies understanding	Negative evaluation ('wrong')
Reflects on paraphrases ideas	Counter proposals, suggestions
Expands on somebody else's idea	Implies judgements (should, should never, you always, everybody ought)

Barnes (1976) has drawn this from Simon and Boyer's (1967 and 1970) work and comments that, 'the "understanding" strategy places responsibility in the learner's hands, reinforcing whatever interpretative framework he/she is able to contribute, whereas "Judging" keeps responsibility in the teacher's hands and, even when positive, places the criteria outside the learner's reach' (Barnes 1976).

ACTION CHECKLIST FOR AGGRESSIVE BEHAVIOUR
There may be times when teachers wish to observe and record socially deviant behaviour of individual pupils. Again, a simple checklist with perhaps timed intervals may be useful. This will enable a profile to be drawn up and out of the analysis may come ideas for dealing with specific behavioural problems. Below is an example checklist provided quoted in *Doing Research* by Rob Walker (1985).

Figure 5.12: Action checklist for aggressive behaviour (Hook 1981)

Behaviour	Time interval (minutes) 0 5 10 15 18
Personal physical attack	
Taunting/ridicule	
Threatening	
Destruction of another pupil's labours	
Usurping property	
etc.	

Alternatively, the checklist could be set out as follows:

Behaviour	No. of occurrences
Personal physical attack	
Taunting/ridicule	
etc.	

MAKE YOUR OWN CHECKLISTS

In making your own checklists you may well take advantage of elements of those designed by others. But it is important to:

1 Identify clearly the purpose.
2 Establish the focus (yourself, a group of children, the class generally or an individual child).
3 Determine the criteria by which you will make judgements on quality and effectiveness.
4 Assess the feasibility. (Can you see it in your own classroom?).
5 Consider issues of validity. (How will/can you check for bias, inference, etc?).
6 Decide on the time frame. (Will you use it for ten minutes, half an hour, a day?).

as well as:

7 Determine the categories.

It will be clear from these examples that teachers have at their disposal a number of means of inquiry into their classrooms; and we have tried to enumerate some of the advantages, disadvantages and uses of these techniques. One which has not yet been discussed is video-recording which while clearly the technique with most potential for learning, may, again at first glance, be most likely to deter teachers because of its cost and potential threat.

Video-recording

Both audio and video recordings allow the teacher to interpret and reinterpret classroom action, allowing new hypotheses to be generated by reflection. They also allow for review by non-participant observers so that a dialogue may be begun. In addition, they provide rich data for retrospective analysis using, for example, observation schedules. Significant incidents can be 'frozen' and replayed, nuances of behaviour can be identified and studied in depth and teachers may observe incidents which they had 'missed' at the time of teaching. Despite the obvious advantages video recording is not widely used as a means of aiding classroom inquiry. It may be that teachers fear self-confrontation, that the video camera is perceived as being too intrusive in the classroom, that equipment is not readily available or that help to operate the equipment is difficult to obtain. Additionally, there are issues of confidentiality, ownership and access which need to be agreed between those who wish to make use of this technique. Our own experience is that where the recording is being used as a result of negotiation between teacher and observer, where teachers believe themselves to be (and are) assisted in the process of self-evaluation (i.e. where the observer is not 'from above') and where they are assured of control of the recording, there is little evidence of stress. Below is an extract from a report of work undertaken with six teachers. Here an outside 'neutral' observer operated a video camera in order to assist each of them in self-evaluation:

(i) *The use of a video camera*
It is important in work of this kind to assess the effect on the participants of the means used (the video camera). Was the video camera intrusive in the

classroom? Did it affect the 'normal' learning situation so much that it constrained the self-evaluation process for the teachers?

Each of the teachers made comments in their diaries about this, and the following typify their responses:

> 'the children, "work as usual, unaffected by the presence of the video"'
> 'although the situation in the classroom while being videoed is never as normal, the children became more relaxed and ignored the camera as more sessions were experienced'
> 'for the most part the children and I seemed unaware of anyone else present. I did not feel the my talking altered in any way because of an "outsider" being present'
> 'the children accepted him as a "friendly visitor" and after the initial interest had waned, they carried on with their normal daily routines, unihibited by the presence of the camera'
> 'the presence of the camera allowed me to become more alert to my own teaching methods and effectiveness'

It is clear that, after the initial session, both teachers and children largely 'forgot' the presence of the camera. The headteacher also commented on this in her written report:

> '...In almost every instance of the video camera's first appearance in the classroom, the teachers were surprised as to how little disruption it caused to the children, who, after an initial spell of interest and curiosity, proceeded to treat the (consultant) as the veritable 'fly on the wall', even to the extent of talking amongst themselves, within his earshot, about subjects not directly related to the task in hand. After two or three visits to a classroom, no more attention appeared to be paid to the video camera, tucked away in a suitable corner, than would be paid to any other piece of static equipment...'

It is worth being careful as one teacher noted, 'not to draw too many conclusions in the early sessions of this kind of work since some children's (and teachers') behaviour may be affected by the presence of a camera operated by a stranger'. This is a classic instance of the problem of reactivity, 'a tendency of any research procedure to distort the reality that it seeks to investigate' (McCormick and James 1983), being recognised and accounted for by the teacher who adopted a reflexive stance to research in which he was engaged.

(Day 1985)

Classroom action research in practice

Finally in this chapter we present a brief example of the way in which classroom action research affected one teacher's thinking and practice.

Thomson and Thomson (1984) contains the accounts of twelve teachers who used an action research approach to improving their practice. Their work was based on the Schools Council's 'Match-Mismatch' materials in which learning experiences and the learning needs of children were compared. The teachers used a variety of techniques to assist them in processes of systematic observation and reflection, and they shared their work with peers through regular meetings. The techniques used included audio-taping, videotaping, and keeping diaries, log books and journals. Below is an extract from one of the accounts by a teacher who used video tape as a reflective tool:

> I set up the video recorder in a corner of my classroom and, following initial teething troubles, I soon learned to have the recorder working within a few minutes. I had used a diary and a cassette recorder before as ways of recording classroom situations, but the video recording was new to me, and also to children, the rest of the staff and the parents. At first all were intrigued by its presence in the classroom. Indeed, after using the camera on many occasions, I am still sometimes conscious of behaving differently when recording, and some of the children do too. Even so I feel the tapes provide a very useful record of what is happening.
>
> I usually focus the camera on a small area of the classroom to record my exchanges with individuals or my contact with small groups of children working together. I also record myself when working with the class group. I told the children, when I introduced them to the idea of the video in the classroom, that it was there to help me to become a more effective teacher. The children made a variety of responses to the presence of the video recorder. Many were indifferent to its presence but several viewed it suspiciously as an 'evil eye', a watchdog looking for signs of bad behaviour. One day I set the equipment to record a girl of 8 painting a picture. Mid-recording, the girl was seen to remove her spectacles. She said afterwards that she felt she would not appear at her best on the tape wearing her spectacles. Most often I used recordings to focus my attention on the quality of my exchanges with individual children to see if this would help me to recognise what the needs of particular children might be.
>
> As the 'Match and Mismatch' meetings continued and we discussed quite openly our different classroom situations, I began to realise that the process of classroom observation had become a part of me – a conscious ongoing part of my daily work. Words and actions that I might have dismissed before, or not even have noticed, took on a new significance. I realised that whether a tape was recording or not I seemed to be observing the classroom as if I was looking at a video re-run.
>
> Before I started my classroom observations with the help of the video, I considered myself to be a good listener. The video helped me to realize that this was not always so. And, more importantly, it helped me to realise how important my listening ability is in my quest to recognise individual needs. In my own defence, I tried to find excuses for my obvious weaknesses, for example, the limited time available to listen to individuals in a working day, my need to be a teacher who surely knew all about the enriching diet a child needs, or the fact that children do not always express their needs in an immediately recognisable form. Two examples from my observations help to illustrate this last point. Through the use of the video I was able to help Peter who had often presented himself as

noisy and disruptive within the classroom. Closer observation showed that this very nervous boy became noisy as a panic response to a new task to which he was not well matched. On another occasion, I looked at a recording of a class discussion we had had about the life and work of Shakespeare. The discussion was interesting and lively though Rebecca, a bright 9-year-old girl, contributed very little. Indeed she often seemed unwilling to reveal her true ability. The impression of Rebecca was confirmed for me on the tape recording. When the discussion ended and the children were going outside, Rebecca passed by me, her friends at some distance. Quietly she told me that she had read and enjoyed the story of Macbeth and that she had a book about Stratford-upon-Avon and Anne Hathaway and much more.

Replaying the tapes is time-consuming but can also be time-saving as so often it gives me new insights about a particular child or confirms previous thinking. It helps me to provide a child with a more appropriate task. The child working at a well-matched task operates independently and works with a will, thus allowing me more time during the classroom hours to look closely at other children and so the process continues.

One evening I sat down to view a tape of James. I had videoed a conversation we had had during the day. James had been working at a table with three other boys all engaged on a similar task. As I noted points about our exchange, I became incidentally aware of Christopher, a bright, timid, hard-working 9-year-old boy. Christopher makes very few demands on me and regrettably, I realised, receives very little of my attention. As I became aware of him on the tape, I realised I knew very little about him. The following short transcript of this video will show how the use of video helped me to understand Christopher a little better.

Five boys are seated around a table getting themselves ready to draw a dead bird they have before them. The children have come together out of interest in the subject. Three of the children are used to getting their own way and are powerful influences in the class groups. They do not dislike Christopher but are indifferent to him.

Christopher: I'm going to draw the legs, hey Jones, I'm going to draw the legs.
Teacher: Christopher, can you come and work round this side of the table?
Peter: James, you hold him up
Christopher: What, round here?
Peter: James, hold it up
Teacher: Do you want the coloured pencils? No, I think sketching pencils will do for now.
Peter: You hold him up, James, and I'll spread out his wings. Eeeee, bird coming into land.

Peter playing with bird and annoying Christopher.

Christopher: I'm going to do the legs
Peter: Look at that colour, look, look shaded kind of
Clive: Look, that feather has come out.
James: Look at that, look at those feathers.
Peter: My God.

James: Look, they run like that

Bird is moved again, though Christopher had settled for second time to sketch.

William: They do they go...
James: You mean they take off like.
Christopher: Ah Clarke, I'm doing the legs.
Peter: They don't half run fast.
Christopher: Ah Jones, I'm drawing the feet.
Clive: You're not now.

Peter and Clive move the bird to suit their purpose and away from Christopher.

Teacher: Which parts have you decided to draw then?
(comes back)
Christopher: I'm drawing the feet
Clive: I'm drawing it sideways
Christopher: I can't see the feet, they keep moving it.

It is several minutes later when the other boys have settled to sketching that Christopher moves his chair to the vantage point he needs and proceeds to produce a beautiful sketch.

I learned so much about Christopher in that ten minutes of tape...'

(Pickover D 1984)

At the beginning of this chapter, we stated that the intention was to provide examples of techniques to assist the individual teacher in processes of classroom review and appraisal through systematic enquiry and to comment upon these. We have asserted the need for self-evaluation by teachers who must be at the heart of any appraisal policy of system which is part of staff development; and that while most teachers do reflect on classroom action as a normal part of their working lives, it will be necessary from time to time for this reflection to become systematic and be made available for public discussion. The implication of this is that the basis of the interpretations and judgements made of data collected from the classroom will have to be made explicit for these to be credible to others. Classroom inquiry thus has three interrelated purposes. In order of priority and importance these are:

1 To enable the teacher to learn more about his or her teaching through reflection and self-confrontation.
2 To enable the teacher to learn more about his or her teaching through sharing this with colleagues.
3 To enable the teacher to justify/explain his or her teaching through sharing with outsiders.

The extent to which teachers and schools achieve these purposes will depend not only on such factors as resources, time and energy, ability, organisational climate and leadership factors but also upon the personal and professional relationships which exist within the school. The quality of these relationships will be expressed implicitly through the organisation and communication structures and, in terms of appraisal and professional development, through the structure and management of the appraisal interview. Our next two chapters focus upon this, and the personal and professional skills which need to be acquired and applied by both appraisor and appraisee if the experience and outcomes are to be of practical benefit to teachers and children.

6 The appraisal interview

There is a great danger that the appraisal interview or performance review will dominate the appraisal scene. Media coverage has placed it at the top of the bill and the teacher's previous interview experiences coupled with feelings of concern over being questioned about practice may combine to produce negative reactions. It is inevitable, therefore, that there will be reservations about the interview based upon those real and perceived fears and the procedural model presented in this chapter takes these into account.

We believe that it should be only a part of the continuous process of collecting information about a teacher's performance and not a substitute for the effective day to day management of staff – and that it should be set firmly in the context of the school's staff development policy. The best definition of the appraisal interview is a 'conversation with a purpose', for it should provide the opportunity for two professionals to discuss all aspects of the teacher's work in an atmosphere which is supportive and constructive with sufficient time available to cover detail. This chapter provides frameworks for organising the preparation, process and outcomes of the interview itself, and the following chapter will consider in detail the skills essential for conducting it. There are two procedural points to be noted by the reader in relation to the approaches used in presenting this chapter. The first concerns the writing style. We have deliberately adopted a more direct personal approach than that used in previous chapters because we want to attempt to represent as closely as possible the preferred ethos of the appraisal interview itself. The second is more complex. Whilst we recognise that, in the main, appraisal interviews are likely to be initiated and managed by staff in senior positions we have tried to provide insights into the feelings of both those being appraised and those who are appraising.

Not everyone finds an interview an enjoyable experience. The whole procedure can be quite worrying, making us feel tense and on edge, sometimes physically sick and even the calm and the casual can suffer from interview nerves. We lie awake at night preparing the perfect answers to those certain questions that everyone tells us we will be asked. Whether we are reviewing our work of the last term or year, or setting targets for the next; or trying for that first promoted post or for a large headship, whether we are successful in our application or whether we live to fight another day 'interview nerves' and worries are something from which we all suffer. Few of us believe that as we walk into that room the rush of the adrenalin around the system is stimulating the brain! Yet there is a different way of looking at the experience where the very thought of an interview excites positive, purposeful feelings in the both appraisor and appraisee.

The purpose of the appraisal interview

When did you last have a couple of hours of uninterrupted time to discuss your job, your high spots, your low spots, your needs and your hopes? The appraisal interview, properly conducted and set against a backcloth of trust, respect, and agreed purposes provides the opportunity for you to discuss your performance at greater length and in greater depth than is normally possible. It will allow you to look back at your performance over the last year and to look forward to work to be done, priorities to be met and targets to be achieved; it will give feed back on progress and development and explore your career aspirations and possible in-service training needs.

At the end of the interview you should have agreed an action plan which will enable you to perform your job as a teacher more effectively, both in the classroom and around the school. It is important not to lose sight of the fact that the whole purpose of appraisal is to develop you and your colleagues as teachers and so improve the quality of the teaching and the learning experiences of our children. Therefore it is right to think . . .

What's in it for me?

- I should have a clear understanding of my job and how well I am doing it and of what is expected of me.
- I should feel secure in the knowledge that my talents are known, appreciated and exploited and that my weaknesses have been identified and constructive help has been offered to improve them.
- I should have discussed my future, including my ambitions and my career prospects, and have received guidance in achieving those aspirations.
- I should feel satisfied that all aspects of my work in and around the school have been discussed in a professional way.
- I should feel happy that everything discussed will be treated in confidence and any written notes will be owned by myself and my interviewer alone.

There are three main elements of the appraisal interview:

1 The preparation.
2 The process.
3 The follow-up.

The preparation

In order that the appraisal interview will be meaningful and helpful it is of paramount importance that, both the interviewer/appraisor and the interviewee/appraisee should attend with an open mind and be adequately prepared. Some consideration, therefore, needs to be given to the following questions:

1. What is the purpose of the interview?
2. When will it be held?
3. Where will it be held?
4. What form will the interview take?
5. What questions will the appraisor ask?
6. What questions will the appraisee ask?
7. What other information, documentation etc. might be required?
8. What do both participants hope to gain from the experience?
9. How will the interview end?
10. How long will the interview take?
11. How will the interview be recorded and what will happen to the interview 'notes'?
12. How will the interview be followed up?

1 *The purpose*

The main purpose of the appraisal interview has been outlined above. Within the primary school situation this will usually be undertaken by the head of the school on an annual basis. Clearly it will have to reflect national and local authority guidelines as well as individual and institutional needs and there should be agreement, preferably in writing, about the objectives of the exercise.

2 *The timing*

Together arrange a convenient time which allows for a satisfactory conclusion to be reached without either of the participants feeling they have been 'rushed' because of other commitments. Finding a two hour slot in the primary teacher's day will be as difficult as finding a two hour slot in the primary headteacher's day! National and local guidelines will, no doubt, offer help here, for finding a lengthy period of unbroken time from the current daily working arrangements will not be easy in the typical primary school.

3 *The venue*

Together arrange an appropriate venue. Thought must be given to privacy and the possibility of interruptions from the telephone and from colleagues and children within the school. The head's room may not be suitable but it is likely to have appropriate furniture such as easy chairs and a low coffee table. The typical headteacher's desk, with the head sitting behind it may not be seen to be appropriate furniture by the appraisee in the interview situation.

Getting the right atmosphere right from the start is vital and knowing that you will be free from interruptions and sitting in comfortable chairs is important. Providing a cup of coffee or tea, (and allowing opportunity for it to be drunk!), will help to create a relaxed atmosphere and create an interpersonal climate conducive to effective interaction described in Chapter 7.

4 *The format*

There should be agreement about the structure of the interview. The introductory stage will clarify the purpose and the areas to be covered, the main part will be devoted to a review of the year and areas for priority development, and the final part will be to agree any plans and targets for the future. These elements will be discussed in more detail later in the chapter.

5/6 *The questions*

It is important that the questions are open-ended and allow the appraisee to do most of the talking. The appraisor should be prepared to listen, rather than ask questions and talk, and give the appraisee opportunity and encouragement to develop any points. The appraisor should ask probing questions in order to check the validity of statements and offer constructive criticism where appropriate. The appraisee should be encouraged to state any views about the school and the staff development process and ask questions too. Both should aim to keep the discussion flowing freely from point to point with a logic which is clear to both.

7 *Supporting information*

It will be appropriate for the appraisee to bring to the interview a copy of any job description, forecasts and records of work, evidence of pupils' progress and the record of the previous interview and agreed targets. A list of extra-curricular activities and in-service training may also be helpful. Any peer appraisal notes, or views from children, could be included.

The appraisor will have similar background information available as well as evidence from classroom observation and of other tasks undertaken where this is appropriate. The appraisor will have also a view of the appraisee's contribution to the life of the school and their career potential.

8 *The gains*

The appraisee should feel that the formal annual review process allows for a full discussion of the year's work in a supportive and constructive environment and that it will pull together all of the 'informal appraisal chats' or progress reviews that will have taken place throughout the year. The appraisor should feel that the opportunity to discuss progress, review the year's work and offer suggestions for development will be helpful to the individual teacher and to the school.

9 The conclusion

The appraisor should bring the interview to a satisfactory conclusion by summarising the main points for action and the time required to achieve the goals and targets which the appraisee and appraisor have agreed. These should be put into writing so that both know what is expected of themselves and the other. This can then be used as a basis for the next review. *It is in a sense a 'contract' for action by both.*

10 The time available

The interviews will take longer than you think! The Suffolk model suggests about two hours and this would seem to be reasonable when considering the agenda. Appraisors should not think of filling the diary for a whole day with appraisal interviews, nor should a commitment precisely two hours after the start of the interviews be contemplated.

11 Recording the interview

It is perfectly reasonable to expect the appraisee and the appraisor to take notes during the interview for they will provide a valuable 'aide-memoire' for agreed action plans. The final written record, having been agreed, should be confidential to the appraisee and the appraisor.

12 Follow-up

The interview is likely to raise a number of areas for action and many of these will be dealt with in the day to day life of the school. It is important to recognise this for it reinforces our view that schools should play the leading part in staff development. Some help with individual requests for in-service training may have to involve the LEA but the major responsibility for developing the individual teacher lies with the school. Promises, and raising expectations, which can never be met, will seriously undermine the whole appraisal process.

The interview process

The success of the appraisal interview will depend very much on the skills of the appraisor to facilitate and exploit the potential of the process and ensure that effective two-way communication takes place. The best appraisals involve the appraisee doing most of the talking – self appraisal with a 'critical friend' – and the appraisor doing most of the listening. But as we suggest in Chapter 7 listening is much more than not speaking so that a wide range of other skills must be brought to the interview to enable successful sharing to take place.

The skills required of the appraisor

These include the ability:

1 to create a positive and supportive atmosphere;
2 to control the pace and direction of the interview;
3 to actively listen;
4 to communicate non-verbally as well as verbally;
5 to lead thinking by questioning;
6 to analyse issues quickly, but refrain from making instant judgements;
7 to clarify thinking and to check on inferences;
8 to select the right time to introduce difficult issues and areas for improvement;
9 to focus on particular issues where there is a concern;
10 to offer praise and encouragement whenever possible;
11 to summarise and reflect as a means of checking that understandings are mutual;
12 to identify goals and targets so that an action plan can be agreed;
13 to provide an agreed written record;
14 to be involved in supportive follow-up activity.

The structure necessary for the interview

In the introductory stage the appraisee and appraisor should:

1 clarify the purpose of the interview – by reviewing progress and development over the last year;
2 outline the areas to be covered – by using the headings and notes on the appraisal comment form (detailed later in the chapter);
3 suggest the format for an agreed written record – by together setting out the targets for next year and how we might tackle them.

In the main stage they should:

1 review the performance of the past year based on the current job description considering those things which have been successful, or not successful, effective or not effective, interesting or not interesting;
2 look at the appraisee's strengths, and consider what use the school has made of them, and those areas that could be improved and developed;
3 consider the problem areas and those where concerns are expressed;
4 give feedback on the above areas;
5 look to the future, identify and seek to agree goals and targets in relation to individual, school, LEA and other perceived needs and agree an appropriate time scale for action;
6 explore any related in-service training needs and career aspirations;
7 offer assistance, where necessary, to meet the goals, targets, training needs and career aspirations.

In the final stage both should:

1 summarise the interview highlighting the main points;
2 agree an action plan and timescale for next year and record it;
3 note any agreed needs and how they might be met.

The range of questions

Open-ended questions allowing the appraisee the opportunity to reflect upon the past year will be more successful than direct questions requiring a 'YES' or 'NO' or a factual statement. The list below is typical of many in use in schools. It would seem to be sensible if both appraisee and appraisor had agreed to the range of questions well before the interview.

1 What are the main tasks and responsibilities of your current post?
2 What parts of your job have given you greatest satisfaction?
3 What parts of your job have given you least satisfaction?
4 What extras, if any, are unclear in your job?
5 Were there any difficulties which prevented you from achieving something you had hoped to do?
6 To help you improve your performance are there any changes in the school organisation which would be beneficial?
7 How can I personally help you more?
8 How would you like to see your career developing next year, and over the next few years?
9 What do you think should be your main target(s) for next year?
10 What help will you need to achieve those targets?

It will be helpful in the long term if the school developed a formal appraisal comment form so that notes could be made systematically as the interview progressed. The headings below suggest an outline which could be followed by the appraisee, prior to the interview, and by both appraisee and appraisor, during the interview.

Table 6.1 Appraisal comment form and summary sheet

1 **Previous appraisal notes**

(a) My targets attained since last appraisal

  (i) Intended

  (ii) Unintended

(b) My targets not attained since last appraisal

(c) Any relevant observations

2 **Myself as a teacher – in the classroom – Discussion points**

(a) My preparation
 (Aims, planning, approaches)

(b) My organisation
 (Resources, environment)

(c) My teaching
 (Presentation, style, match of work, pace, progression)

(d) My relationships
 (Personal, social, educational, individual children)

(e) My follow-up work
(Marking, recording, feedback, evaluation)

3 Myself as a teacher – around the school

(a) My curriculum involvement

(b) My co-operation and participation

(c) My extra-curricular work

4 Myself as a teacher – in the community

(a) My involvement with parents

(b) My involvement with other supporting agencies

5 Myself as a manager

(a) My management skills

(b) My leadership skills

(c) My own professional development

6 **My Future Needs**
(a) In-Service Training

(b) New experiences

(c) Career aspirations

(d) My potential

7 **Our agreed plan for next year**

    Target   Resources required   Timescale   Strategy

8 **Our agreed summary of discussion and appraisal of performance**

DATE _____   APPRAISEE _____

                                          APPRAISOR _____

The follow-up

Such a comment form would be confidential to the appraisee and the appraisor and should be kept safe, at least until the next appraisal interview. The form could be used, with agreement, as a record of a teacher's progress over a number of years and could be the basis of a Teacher Profile. Certainly the information from the in-service training section would be valuable in this respect.

It is important that action follows the interview. It may be that some activities can be undertaken almost immediately as part of the day to day work of the school and this will give confidence to the appraisee as words are translated into deeds. It is inevitable that expectations will have been raised and any long delays will result in frustration and cynicism if there is no sign of the help or support materialising. Hints of promotion or the possibility of a long secondment or a transfer to another school to widen experience should not be part of the feedback process. The appraisor should be confident that the targets agreed are capable of being attained within the timescale and should not rely on the LEA to fulfil any of the targets unless provisions have already been made.

A good staff development programme will take account of the individual teacher's needs alongside those of the school. A sensible professional development profile with appropriate experience might well lead to a promotion. A re-training requirement for the teacher and the school might lead to a secondment and would certainly need the co-operation of the LEA; similarly the LEA would need to be involved at an early stage in any transfer request. As schools and LEAs make long-term plans for development then each school will get to know the processes and opportunities available and can actively consider their best use.

The appraisal interview provides the means for a formal review of the year's work but it must not replace the regular informal chats which are an essential part of the daily life of the typical primary school. Waiting for a year to be 'developed' is not helpful to the teacher or to the class of children. It is through the formal and informal processes of professional interaction that the key benefits of appraisal are to be derived. The appraisal interview has the potential to be a powerful learning experience for both the appraisor and the appraisee. A well managed interview can raise professional awareness, deepen understanding, present insights, increase motivation and facilitate professional development; and the next chapter considers the kinds of attitudes and skills which are needed if these are to be achieved.

7 Personal and professional relationships

In order to engage successfully with colleagues in the kinds of appraisal activities outlined in the previous chapters it is important to focus on the nature and quality of personal and professional relationships. This chapter will look specifically at relationships and behaviour and at the implications of these in the management of appraisal and professional development. It has already been stressed how vital good teamwork is to the achievement of successful educational outcomes. Schools which pay scant attention to personal and professional relationships run the risk of inhibiting the realisation of the enormous creative potential present, individually and collectively, in the staff of a primary school. One of the greatest challenges in school management is that of unlocking this potential and making it available for school development and growth. Unfortunately other priorities have tended to preoccupy the management processes in schools.

Although the schooling system suffers from an intrinsic resistance to change, attempts to modify it have concentrated in two main areas, and it is with these that school management has been concerned. Firstly, there has developed a belief that if only the structural problems of schooling can be solved, effective and efficient education will result. Changes such as the raising of the school leaving age and comprehensive organisation have not realised the hopes expected of them. The move towards a first, middle and secondary school organisation enjoyed some popularity until falling rolls created problems of economy and viability. Secondly, there has been an accompanying belief that the allocation of considerable resources to curriculum research and design would result in more relevant and satisfying learning in schools. This has not proved to be true as the evidence referred to in Chapter 3 shows. Primary schools today are very similar to what they were forty years ago.

This preoccupation with the structures and the curriculum of education has resulted in a failure to take account of a possible third way to progress – the climate of schooling. This relates to considerations such as personality, relationships, interactions, values, hopes, feelings and behaviours. In both the structure of schooling and in the design of the curriculum there has been a disregard for the pupil as a person, attempting to learn in a society abounding in contradictions and inconsistencies. For many pupils, schooling has been a crushing rather than a liberating experience. This failure to see the central importance of personality and personhood has extended to teachers as well as pupils. Management structures built on hierarchies and autocratic decision making have failed to activate and release professional potential in teachers and the move towards more participatory methods has been slow to transform traditional attitudes to power and authority.

School management built on the concept of person centredness would place a high priority on the quality of life within the organisation, both among pupils and teachers. Promoting the teamwork factors listed on page 42 would do much to build a realisation among teachers of their great capacity to contribute in a co-managing role to the development of the school.

Some key concepts

In attempting to determine a more person centred approach to school management it is necessary to give attention to some of the factors which affect and influence behaviour and performance, and which play a crucial part in establishing relationships.

Human potential

Central to the idea of person centredness is the concept of human potential. This suggests that living is a process of becoming – a gradual unfolding of personhood. Leading humanistic psychologists, such as Abraham Maslow and Carl Rogers, have argued that individuals have within themselves vast resources for healthy and successful living. These resources become minimalised and supressed during the process of socialisation but can be rekindled if a supportive psychological climate is provided. Such an actualizing tendency is a characteristic of human beings but is also present in all living organisms. Classrooms have tended not to be psychologically safe for this process of growth and unfolding in pupils, and staffrooms do not provide the psychological climate in which this directional process can be promoted and celebrated. Just as many pupils leave school thwarted and unfulfilled, so many teachers carry on their day to day business in a professional atmosphere characterised by anxiety, mistrust and frustration. And this may be exacerbated by the imposition of appraisal interviews which are for the benefit of the head and not the teacher.

The process of appraisal needs to consider to what extent the climate of the school provides conditions for human growth, and the extent to which supposed under performance can be attributed to the undernourishing quality of the human environment. Successful management is very much a process of activating potential and of providing space and conditions in which it can creatively be expressed. One of the priority aims for headteachers should be the cultivation of the actualizing tendency in themselves and in each and every member of staff.

One of the outcomes of the analytical processes outlined in the previous chapters should be an increased awareness of the ways that the organisational factors – values, authority and relationships – combine to enhance or diminish human potential. In order to understand the surface characteristics of an organisation it is necessary to look below its surface as suggested by the Iceberg Theory referred to in Chapter 3.

Self concept

The self concept refers to the collection of ideas, attitudes, and beliefs about ourselves that inhabit self awareness at any moment. In other words it is about the kind of person we see ourselves as being. In addition to ideas and thoughts about who we are, we also have feelings about our perceived identity. This is sometimes referred to as self-esteem – the extent to which we like, value and respect ourselves as people.

Within any organisation there will be considerable differences, as well as some similarities of self concept. These will depend upon each individual's:

- level of self awareness;
- intellectual response to that awareness;
- emotional response to that awareness.

A strong and positive self concept is conducive to healthy growth and development and necessary if effective working relationships are to be established. A poor or negative self concept can generate feelings of insecurity and a general sense of unworthiness. Clearly then, attention to the self concept is a very important part in the management process of building a person centred organisation. Some aspects of the self concept are particularly important where teamwork is being developed (Elliott-Kemp 1982):

1	Self awareness	The extent to which we are aware of our own attitudes and values and of the effect our own behaviour has on others.
2	Will to achieve	the extent to which we seek new challenges in our work and personal lives.
3	Optimism	the extent to which we feel positive about the future and our part in it.
4	Positive regard	the extent to which we respond to others with warmth, caring and respect.
5	Trust	the extent to which we are prepared to place trust in those with whom we work.
6	Congruence	the extent to which we are secure enough to be ourselves with our colleagues.
7	Empathy	the extent to which we are able to understand the circumstances of our colleagues lives from their point of view.
8	Courage	the extent to which we are prepared to take risks in finding more effective ways of working with colleagues and the extent to which we are prepared to admit to a need for help from them.

128 *Appraisal and professional development in the primary school*

When these qualities are well developed in the individual members of a working group then teamwork is likely to be of a high order. The person centred school is one which not only focuses on developing the self concept of pupils but one which attaches high importance to the self concepts of staff. It works towards creating conditions in which these particular considerations are given space and time to develop. When the self concept of a particular teacher is low it is in the interests of all other colleagues to be concerned.

Motivation

One of the most important yet challenging tasks of school management is the creating of a high motivational climate. Motivation is the process of responding to inner needs and drives. While individuals will have needs that are particular and specific they will also have needs in common with all other members of staff. Within the organisational setting of a school five sets of needs have especial importance. These are:

1 A sense of belonging.
2 A sense of achievement.
3 A sense of appreciation.
4 A sense of influence.
5 A sense of ownership.

Such motivation factors are central to appraisal and staff development and successful teamwork will depend upon creating conditions in which these particular needs are focused on. Herzberg (1966) has suggested that in organisations workers are also highly motivated when:

1 The work itself is intrinsically satisfying and challenging.
2 Workers have a decision making role and are involved in the management of the organisation.
3 Successful work leads to the possibility of promotion.

He also discovered that workers are badly motivated when:

1 They are oversupervised and there are too many rules and regulations governing personal as well as professional activity.
2 Workers have difficult relationships with senior staff and when 'bossy' attitudes cause frustration and anxiety.
3 There are poor relationships with co-workers, poor staff morale and divisive attitudes.
4 The working conditions are poor.

This emphasises how important it is to be person centred and to pay attention to the human factors of the organisation. It is also vital to balance this with a high sense of purpose through the identifying of specific tasks and objectives and the clear definition of roles and responsibilities.

Empowerment

This is a concept closely related to the actualising tendency referred to above. It concerns the capacity of individuals to take increasing responsibility for the satisfying of their personal and professional needs. It differs from motivation in that empowerment places the emphasis upon the individual for creating his or her own conditions for growth, for defining challenges and for setting goals and targets. Central to this concept are a number of key assumptions and values (Hopson and Scally 1981). These include:

1. Each person is a unique individual worthy of respect.
2. Individuals are responsible for their own actions and behaviour.
3. Individuals are responsible for their own feelings and emotions and for their responses to the behaviour of others.
4. New situations, however unwelcome, contain opportunities for new learning and growth.
5. Mistakes are learning experiences and are seen as outcomes rather than failures.
6. The seeds of our own growth are within us. Only we ourselves can activate our potential for creativity and growth.
7. We can all do more than we are currently doing to become more than we currently are.
8. Awareness brings responsibility and responsibility creates the opportunity for choice.
9. Our own fear is the major limiter to our growth.
10. Growth and development never end. Self empowerment is not an end to be achieved but a constant process of becoming.

Within organisations those who operate in a self empowered way are characterised by:

1. An acceptance that change and development are the natural order of things and that change is to be welcomed rather than shunned and avoided.
2. Having the skills to initiate change and the capacity to learn new skills and ideas.
3. Taking personal responsibility for actions and behaviour.
4. Making clear goals for themselves and developing action programmes to meet them.
5. Being action biased.
6. Frequently reviewing, assessing and evaluating their own progress and seeking feedback from others.
7. Being concerned to see others taking greater responsibility for their own lives.

The kinds of self and peer appraisal through action research described in Chapters 4 and 5 build upon rather than act against these characteristics. In the successful school, characterised by good teamwork, many teachers will be operating in a self empowered way. In such a school, appraisal becomes a process of facilitating this process, of providing regular opportunities for review and evaluation and the provision of regular feedback. Attempting to create a climate which is person centred, motivating and empowering is a vital challenge to those involved in school leadership. The pursuit of such positive ideas is likely to avoid the situation described by Lieberman and Hardie (1981):

> There is a lot of pain in human systems that doesn't have to be there. There is a lot of hope, aliveness and joy ready to flower when the members of the system can learn how to nourish these positive qualities.

Locus of control

A further insight into behaviour within organisations is offered by the concept of 'locus of control'. Rotter (1966) suggests that it is possible to distinguish two particular control dynamics. The first of these identifies those people who feel very much in charge of themselves and agents of their own destinies as 'internals' – their locus of control is within themselves. Those who feel that they have very little control over what happens to them are referred to as 'externals' – their locus of control is perceived as being external to themselves. Evidence by J.E. Phares (1976) makes it very clear that those who operate their lives with an 'internal' dynamic are better able to make choices in their life, take responsibility for their own actions and the consequences of them and are better able to cope with failure and learn successfully from it. In particular Phares discovered that 'internals':

1. Have greater self control;
2. are better at retaining information;
3. ask more questions of people;
4. notice more of what is happening around them;
5. are less coercive when given power;
6. see other people as being responsible for themselves;
7. prefer activities requiring skill than those involving chance;
8. have higher academic achievements;
9. are more likely to delay gratification;
10. accept more responsibility for their own behaviour;
11. have more realistic reactions to their own successes and failures;
12. are less anxious;
13. exhibit less pathological behaviour.

The clear implications from research work in the area of 'locus of control' is that when people accept responsibility for themselves and their own behaviour and recognise their own power to affect and influence the way that circumstances develop, they will be likely to work more creatively and co-operatively to the benefit of the organisation as a whole. Within the school setting and in the context of appraisal there is a clear need to identify and cultivate an 'internal' dynamic both within the classrooms of the school and in the staffroom. The research also provides guidance for leaders. The 'internal' dynamic is likely to be developed in an organisational climate characterised by warmth, protection and nurturance.

Listening

The curriculum in schools has always demonstrated a preoccupation with language and communication. Unfortunately the concern has been overwhelmingly directed at the two processes least to do with interpersonal communication – reading and writing. Talking and listening have never featured as key elements in the language programmes of most schools and it is often the case today that language learning is still conducted in silence. The almost total neglect of listening as a subject for attention within the school curriculum was reinforced by HMI in the discussion document *English from 5-16: Curriculum Matters 1*. The document sets the context for language learning very well:

> It is the principle means by which we think, define what we experience and feel, and interpret the world in which we live; and the principle means by which we communicate with other people.

What the document fails to provide support for, or give guidance in are the sorts of classroom learning experiences that make such a process of definition and interpretation possible. It is through the process of interpersonal communication that we bring meaning to our many and varied experiences and yet inside classrooms the opportunity for pupils to engage in structured talk about their learning, and about their personal experiences is almost totally absent. The document proposes that:

> Talking, listening, reading and writing, should constantly and naturally interrelate... to ensure that all four modes occur in appropriate proportion.

However, there seems to be an almost complete misunderstanding of what listening really is. Within the document it is regarded more as a method of filtering sound than a key ingredient in human relationships.

Those of us now engaged in the business of providing language learning experiences in classrooms need to be aware that we have ourselves been deprived of that most crucial opportunity – learning how to become effective listeners. In most classrooms children are urged to listen, sometimes to 'listen harder' yet rarely is time and opportunity provided to teach them how to do it.

Being good at receiving messages, in appraisal interviews for example, is closely linked to our skills as listeners. One of the key qualities of highly facilitative teachers has been shown to be that of having the ability to be a good listener (Aspy and Roebuck 1976). As one of the key factors in effective communicating, listening has not only been neglected by the schooling system, it has not featured as a key element in the initial training of teachers. Not only is it important for teachers (who probably spend more time talking to pupils than listening to them) to practise and develop active listening skills, but it is equally important that pupils have the opportunity to build on a listening capability which is naturally present in their infancy, but which tends to diminish through the process of socialisation and schooling.

With so little attention having been paid to listening it is important to establish a working definition.

132 *Appraisal and professional development in the primary school*

> Listening is an active and dynamic process in which the listener attempts to gain insights into the perceptual, intellectual and emotional world of the speaker.

So far from being the passive activity suggested by HMI, listening is seen to be a very active and practical skill.

For the purposes of this chapter, listening is regarded in the context of the set of skills used by the appraiser in the appraisal interview to help the appraisee to talk openly and freely about the issues under consideration. For the interview to be successful there is an increased responsibility on the appraiser to display effective listening behaviour. While improved listening skills will benefit all human interactions they are particularly essential in the sort of professional relationship where it is important for one of the partners to share perceptions, concerns, worries and frustrations, and for the other to be the helper, listening to and encouraging the other to explore the issues and concerns.

The capacity to be a good listener depends upon the appropriate use of a cluster of certain key skills:

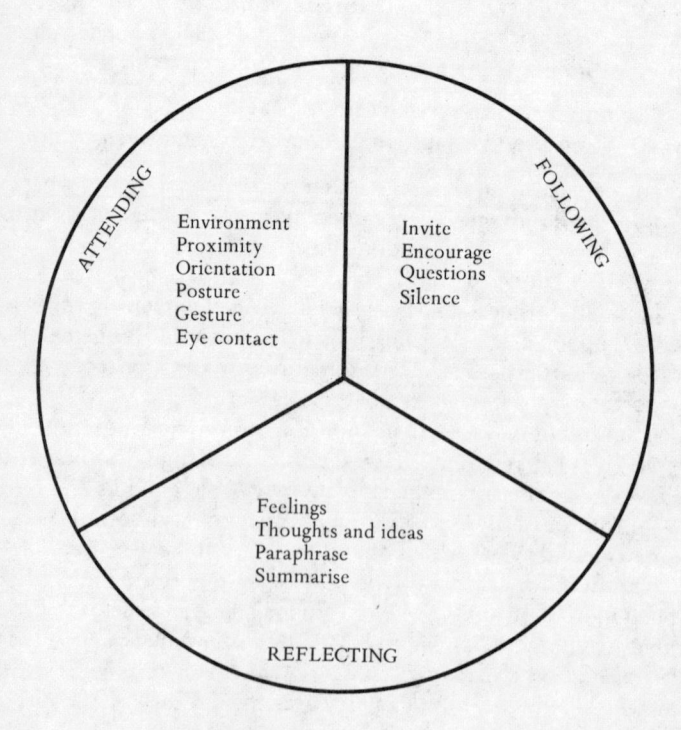

Figure 7.1: The skills of active listening

Attending

This initial cluster is concerned with establishing the right conditions for an effective interaction. Conveying a sense of active attention to the appraisee requires:

1 an environment as free from distraction as possible;
2 sitting reasonably close to each other;
3 chairs set at a slight angle to each other;
4 leaning slightly foreward in a posture of involvement;
5 conscious use of appropriate gestures and facial expression;
6 good eye contact.

These actions and behaviours help to create an interpersonal climate conducive to effective interaction. They convey to the teacher being appraised a sense of the appraisor's commitment to the task, of having time to listen and being interested and concerned in the teacher's affairs.

Following

Once a suitable climate has been created it is necessary to get the teacher talking and to encourage ideas and feelings to be expressed. The cluster of skills required here include:

1 Inviting the speaker to talk – 'Would you like to start by telling me about your work so far this term?'
2 Encouraging the speaker to keep talking – 'Could you say a little more about that?'
3 Using limited questions.
4 Keeping an attentive silence.

All these factors are to do with creating the sort of environment in which the appraisee feels safe to disclose difficulties and problems as well as to share successes and achievements. Once the teacher has begun to talk it is important to keep the talk going so that matters that need to be brought out are done so. This means good non-verbal communication and some minimal verbal responding. It is difficult to avoid the temptation to intervene and take the agenda away from the talker. Maintaining an attentive silence is the key skill to cultivate if this is to be avoided.

The best way to develop these listening skills of attending and following is to try and change the balance of talking to listening in our interpersonal communications, particularly with those who seek out our help. Far too often we use the time when we should be listening to rehearse in our own minds what we are going to say next. Really effective listening involves an increased capacity to concentrate on the other person's interests and concerns. In conversation listening and talking are of equal importance to both participants. In the appraisal relationship and other helping contexts, listening has an altogether more important function.

Reflecting

This final cluster of skills involves conveying to the speaker a sense of being understood. This requires:

1 Reflecting the speaker's feelings.
2 Reflecting the speaker's thoughts and ideas.
3 Paraphrasing what has been said.
4 Summarising from time to time.

It is facility with this cluster of skills that makes the difference between active, effective listening and merely hearing. When the speaker truly gets the feeling that the listener is really interested, is prepared to stay with the talker's subject and not to intervene in a judgmental way, then effective communication can be said to have occurred.

The improving of listening skills is a systematic and painstaking process. Training in workshop conditions, where specific skills can be focused upon and feedback provided by observers, can be very beneficial for most and essential for some. Appraisal interviews will never become valued experiences if they are used by the appraiser as a means of dealing with their own worries and concerns.

Empathy

In addition to the cluster of skills which make for effective listening, it is important for the appraiser to behave with warmth, care and sensitivity. The behaviours which convey those feelings can be summarised by the word empathy. The concept of empathy is central to effective communication. In general terms this is the ability to convey to other people an understanding of their problems and feelings. It involves the sensing of the emotions of those we set out to try and help and being able to communicate this sensing to them. Basically it stems from being a good listener and responding with sensitivity and understanding.

In attempting to increase the capacity for empathy it is necessary to recognise two aspects:

1 Receiving: receiving messages from the other person and from them being able to sense the emotions involved.
2 Reflecting: being able to convey this sensing back to the other person.

Ability in the first of these aspects is demonstrated through the second. In other words understanding is conveyed through the form of the responding. Being empathetic is a matter of using communication skills to test out the validity of the interpretation that is placed on the other's message. In the analysis of listening outlined above it is the first two clusters of skills – attending and following – that are to do with receiving the message and the third cluster – reflecting – that is to do with the conveying of a sense of understanding.

Introducing empathetic responding into our repertoire of communication skills can be difficult. Instead of the give and take that characterises most of our interactions we are more concerned in empathetic responding with giving back to the speaker what has been offered, rather than adding something. The skill comes in the way that the reflective response is phrased. In the following interaction the headteacher is merely echoing the actual words of the teacher:

Teacher I'm not getting anywhere with these applications.
Headteacher You're not getting anywhere with your applications.
Teacher I'm obviously being too ambitious.
Headteacher You're obviously being too ambitious.

The essential quality of empathetic responding is conveying to the other person that their feelings and emotions have been sensed correctly. In the above example all that the headteacher has done is demonstrate that the words that the teacher has used have been remembered. A more empathetic head might have handled the situation as follows:

Teacher I'm not getting anywhere with these applications.
Headteacher It sounds as if you are very frustrated about that.
Teacher Yes, I'm obviously being too ambitious.
Headteacher So you are not really capable of doing the jobs you have applied for?

In this example the head is determined to stay with the teacher's problem. By reflecting back what has been said, the head is helping the teacher to come to terms with her feelings about not getting promotion. This involves staying on the teacher's subject matter until the feelings have been brought out and sufficiently explored. Only then can possible coping strategies and plans for action be considered.

In an appraisal interview between a head and a member of staff, the importance of empathetic responding cannot be overemphasised. It is particularly crucial early in an interaction when the establishing of rapport and the developing of trust determines the eventual success of the interview.

To avoid the mechanical responding of the headteacher in the first example quoted above, it is useful to develop a range of responding styles. Apart from those used in the second example the following can also be tried:

'What I think you are saying is...'
'If I have understood you correctly...'
'From your point of view...'
'Correct me if I am wrong, but...'
'So, as you see it...'

The greatest temptation in the listening role is to convey to the speaker what the concern looks like from our own point of view. In many situations giving our own opinions can lead to further frustration, with the other person feeling increasingly misunderstood. Essentially, empathetic responses are designed to show the speaker that we are trying to understand what is being said, that we accept how the speaker feels, and that we are sensing what the problem looks like from his or her point of view.

Learning to behave in an empathetic way involves attention to certain key strategies:

1 Frequently checking out that we have accurately sensed how the other person is

feeling.
2 Watching out for both verbal and non verbal signals that offer insights.
3 Listening for the meanings and feelings expressed in the words.
4 Being sensitive to changes of feeling and meaning.
5 Being able to enter the perceptual world of the other person and being at home in it.

Counselling skills and appraisal

All of the ideas about listening and empathy mentioned above feature in the training of counsellors and psychotherapists. There is an increasing demand among teachers for training in counselling skills and this will certainly be beneficial to pupils. Headteachers too, finding themselves increasingly involved in dealing with social, marital and family issues, as well as purely educational ones, are also seeking opportunities to acquire the skills essential to the counsellor. If appraisal is to be successful in improving the quality of learning in schools and extending the professional skills of teachers then consideration needs to be given to how counselling skills might benefit the relationship of appraiser and appraisee.

Let us first be clear what counselling is, since the term is frequently misused and the activity misunderstood. Counselling has been defined by Francesca Inskipp (1985) as:

1 Providing help and support for someone who is concerned or perplexed.
2 Creating a safe and accepting climate so that the other person can talk freely and openly about problems and their associated feelings.
3 Helping the other person to gain insights into problems and concerns so as to generate practical solutions to them.

Counselling works from the assumption that those with problems and anxieties have the resources to deal with them quite adequately themselves but that help is needed if those resources are to be activated. Most of the time when people share their problems they are not seeking advice, the offering of solutions or even reassurance. They simply want to be heard, to have their point of view acknowledged and their feelings accepted. Most of us in the course of our lives have become so used to being offered other people's solutions to personal anxieties and concerns that our own problem solving skills have never fully been developed. (Hendricks & Hendricks 1985).

Counselling is a client centred activity in which the counsellor has no vested interest in the outcomes which the client achieves. This is not so in the professional relationships that exist among the staff of a school. Here status differentials create differences and expectations that make the strict counselling relationship both impossible and inappropriate. For this reason it is important to recognise that counselling in its strict sense cannot be part of the process of appraisal and professional development. What is appropriate is to consider some of the features of the counselling relationship which have a positive contribution to make to the management processes of the school. Carl Rogers, the originator of client centred counselling, advocates the development of three particular qualities as being essential in the effective counsellor. These are:

1 empathy;
2 warmth;
3 genuineness.

The first of these has already been dealt with above.

Warmth

Rogers used the phrase 'unconditional positive regard' to describe the warm, caring respect the counsellor needs to have for the client. Murgatroyd summarises Rogers's thinking as:

1 A person in need comes to you for help.
2 If they are to be helped they need to know that you will understand their problems and feelings.
3 Whatever your own feelings about who they are and what they have done, you will accept them as they are.
4 If they sense that you are understanding and accepting of them they will be able to disclose their concerns and problems and be open to the possibilities of change and development.
5 If, however, they feel that you have a vested interest in their change and the relationship is conditional upon that, then they may experience pressure and reject the help.

(Murgatroyd 1985).

Genuineness

Rogers believed that effective counselling becomes possible when the counsellor communicates in an open and direct way with the client. Once a role posture is adopted, authenticity becomes lost and the relationship suffers. This means that the counsellor has to be as open about thoughts and feelings as the client is expected to be. When this happens a genuineness communicates itself to the client and the relationship grows.

Feedback

Part of a good appraisal interview is the providing of feedback to teachers on their work. This is an important but also potentially hazardous operation. Handled badly the giving of feedback can undermine confidence, lower self-esteem and reinforce negative attitudes. A very useful theoretical device to emphasise the importance of feedback is the Jo-Hari Window. (See Figure 7.2).

This conceptual model of the human personality is named after its originators - Jo Luft and Harry Ingham. The sectors within the frame represent all that is known about us, either by ourselves or by others. Self awareness is increased when we are successful in penetrating the 'blind' area but also when through sharing more of ourselves with others we begin to diminish the 'hidden' area and thereby appreciate

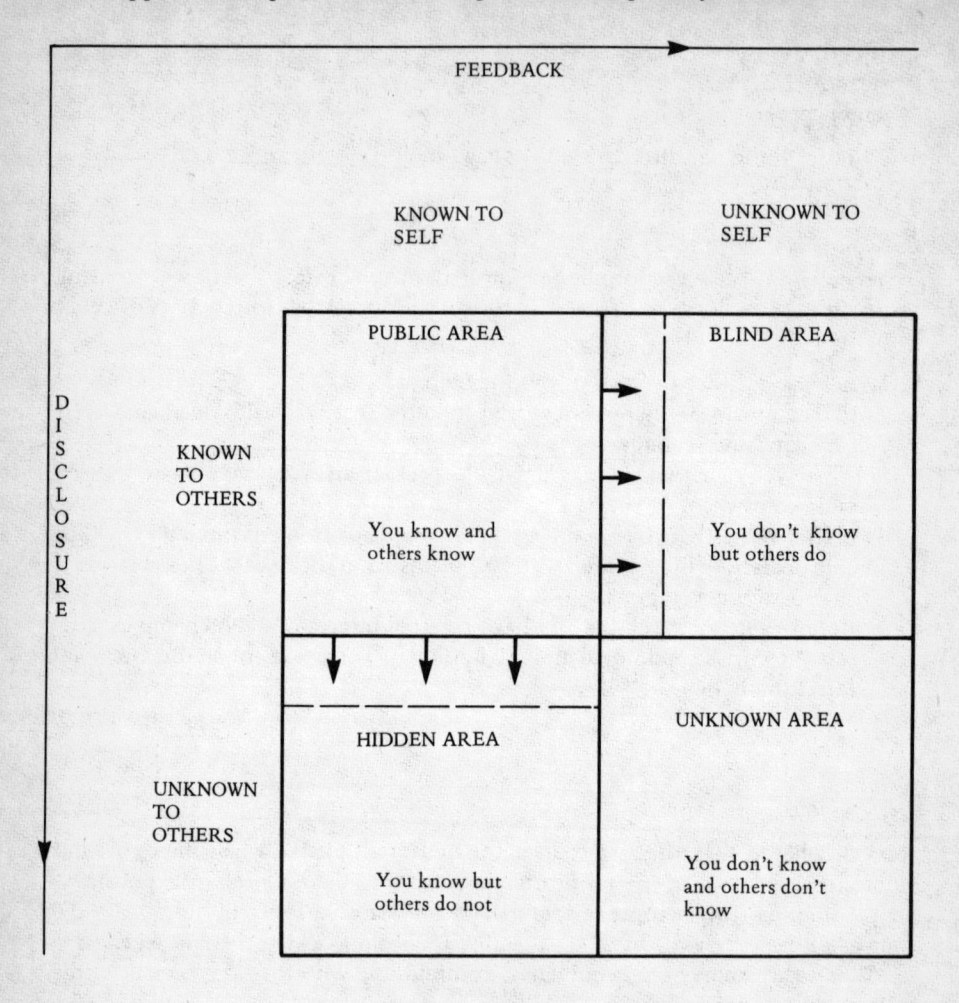

138 *Appraisal and professional development in the primary school*

```
                              FEEDBACK →

                    KNOWN TO              UNKNOWN TO
                    SELF                  SELF

                    ┌─────────────────┬─────────────────┐
                    │  PUBLIC AREA    │  BLIND AREA     │
                    │                 │                 │
        KNOWN       │                 │                 │
D       TO          │                 │                 │
I       OTHERS      │ You know and    │ You don't know  │
S                   │ others know     │ but others do   │
C                   │                 │                 │
L                   ├─────────────────┼─────────────────┤
O                   │  HIDDEN AREA    │  UNKNOWN AREA   │
S                   │                 │                 │
U       UNKNOWN     │                 │                 │
R       TO          │                 │ You don't know  │
E       OTHERS      │ You know but    │ and others don't│
                    │ others do not   │ know            │
                    └─────────────────┴─────────────────┘
↓
```

Figure 7.2: The Jo-Hari Window (Luft and Ingham)

the greater potential in our own lives. To increase awareness of ourselves we need to pursue experiences which:

1 provide opportunities for disclosure;
2 provide opportunities to receive feedback on our own behaviour.

It is with the second of these with which we are now concerned. If it is to be helpful feedback needs to be given in a supportive way as Table 7.1 suggests.

The listening skills outlined above should also be remembered before undertaking appraisal feedback. Particularly important is the process of reflecting, checking that

Table 7.1: Giving feedback

Try to	*Try not to*
1 Comment on and discuss specific incidents and events – about what has actually been done or said.	Comment on and discuss what the person is like, their motives, shortcomings or seeming inadequacies.
2 Deal with what has been observed and heard.	Deal with what has been assumed or inferred.
3 Use descriptions.	Use judgements.
4 Be specific.	Be general.
5 Deal with what is immediate and recent.	Deal with incidents and events from the past.
6 Share ideas and information.	Give advice and provide clear cut solutions.
7 Comment on behaviours that can reasonably be changed and developed.	Raise unreasonable expectations for change.
8 Deal with issues which will benefit the receiver.	Deal with issues for your own satisfaction.
9 Limit feedback to a few key observations the receiver can do something about.	Overload the receiver with criticisms that confuse and frustrate the receiver.

what the receiver has heard is what you meant. Occasional summaries are useful to keep track of key points and the session should end with an agreed summary of the whole session.

Non-verbal communication

In human interactions the majority of information about the other person tends to be communicated non-verbally. Any consideration of personal and professional relationships must therefore give attention to this important phenomenon. Eight forms of non-verbal communication have been shown to be particularly significant (Argyle 1983).

1 Facial expression

The main function of facial expression is to communicate emotional states and convey attitudes of liking or disliking. Most of us can quickly recognise facial expressions which suggest happiness, surprise, fear, sadness, anger, disgust, and interest. The mouth and eyebrows are particularly significant in creating specific expressions but each state also involves a configuration of the whole face. Facial expressions tend to be used as social signals as well as indicators of emotions. Most people are fairly aware of their expressions and can control them, although 'leakage' does occur when the emotions involved are particularly strong.

2 Gaze

This is the principal means of gathering non-verbal information but also functions as a social signal itself. Eye contact is a very important feature of interpersonal relationships and we tend to engage in more eye contact with those we like. It is also used as a device to synchronise speech.

3 Gestures

Movements of hand, body and head are closely co-ordinated with speech and are used to add emphasis to what is being said. They can also be indicative of emotional states.

4 Bodily posture

Each of us tends to have a characteristic repertoire of bodily movements but postures do provide some information about how tense or relaxed a person is and may indicate something about self image, self confidence and emotional state.

5 Bodily contact

This is is controlled by strict rules in our culture and is mainly focused in family relationships and between lovers. However there are a range of socially acceptable touching rituals often to do with greeting and departing. Informal touching between friends and as a means of encouragement and reinforcement seems to be on the increase with a relaxation of some traditional taboos.

6 Spacial behaviour

Proximity is an indication of intimacy in most relationships and also relates to the degree of formality in interactions. Orientation of chairs in relationships can also have an effect on the nature and quality of interactions. Generally speaking chairs placed at an angle of about 45° make for the most conducive arrangement, facilitating sufficient eye contact to sustain effective interaction.

7 Clothes and appearance

Although social expectations about dress are more relaxed than they once were what we wear is an important part of social behaviour. Our clothes and appearance can be manipulated to some extent and can be used to convey information about status, occupation, and class; and also attitudes to other people like rebelliousness or conformity. This category is more susceptible to changing fashions than the others mentioned here.

8 Voice

This form of non-verbal behaviour refers to tone of voice, speed of talking, timing, accent and inclination to talk or to keep silent.

Non-verbal communication functions in four specific ways (Argyle 1975):

1 Communicating interpersonal attitudes and emotions.
2 Self presentation.
3 Ritual.
4 Supporting verbal communication.

Each of these non-verbal behaviours can be seen at work in most organisations and it is important to be aware of just how powerful an effect they have on the psychological climate of the school as a whole and upon particular relationships. The vital point to remember is that it is not *WHAT* we do that matters as much as the *WAY* that we do it. In other words, the particular combination of non-verbal behaviours that we exhibit is likely to have a more powerful effect on those we work with than any other aspect of ourselves. For those in leadership positions it is essential to have a high degree of self awareness about non-verbal behaviours and to pay attention to to them when conducting appraisal discussions, helping colleagues with problems and making presentations at meetings. There is a growing literature in the whole field of interpersonal communication and it is now recognised that the most effective and successful organisations are those where, amongst other things, there is a high level of personal and interpersonal awareness and where there is a high degree of trust and openness in interactions (Peters and Waterman 1982).

Barriers to communication

As well as positive communication and relationship behaviours to develop through practice there are certain dangers to avoid. Some verbal strategies frequently result in effective communication becoming frustrated (Nelson-Jones 1986).

1 Directing and leading

This is where the appraiser takes control of what the colleague wants to talk about:

> 'I think we should talk about the difficulties you seem to be having with your topic work.'
> 'Let's leave that and go on to your special responsibility work.'
> 'I'd rather concentrate on what you think you have achieved than get distracted by what has gone wrong.'

2 Judging and evaluating

This involves making evaluative statements and often implies a failure to live up to certain standards, usually the appraisor's.

> 'That seems a very unwise choice of topic.'
> 'You certainly made a real mess of that assembly.'
> 'You don't seem to be able to organise your groupwork at all well.'

3 Blaming

Pointing the finger and assigning responsibility in a scapegoating way.

> 'It wouldn't have happened without your intemperate interruption.'
> 'You've landed me with a real problem now.'
> 'No wonder the reading results are so poor this year.'

4 Getting aggressive

Making statements that are hurtful and demeaning and likely to put the other person down.

> 'Dont come to me with that excuse again.'
> 'But just how many times do I have to tell you?'
> 'You really are hopeless.'

5 Moralising and preaching

Telling the other person how they should be living, conveyed in a patronising way.

> 'You are the deputy head, I don't expect that of you.'
> 'We can't expect the children to do it right if we don't set an example.'
> 'That is simply not the way we do things in this school.'

6 Advising

Offering solutions and not allowing the other to work towards solutions of their own.

> 'I should go back to the original plan and forget this new idea.'
> 'You need to spend much more time on preparation.'
> 'You need to go on a few courses before you can think about promotion.'

7 Denying feelings

Not accepting the other person's feelings.

Personal and professional relationships 143

'I'm sure its not as bad as you make out.'
'Come on, don't get so depressed about it.'
'Of course you're not inadequate.'

8 Stealing the agenda

Taking the subject away from the other person and talking about yourself.

'You think you have a problem. Wait until you hear mine.'
'Yes, I had a situation like that once and I can tell you exactly what to do.'
'Ah! Have I told you about the time that happened to me?'

9 Interrogating

Asking excessive questions in an aggressive and intrusive manner.

'Have you got a problem at home?'
'Where on earth did you get that suit from?'
'You'd better tell me what is going on between you.'

10 Reassuring

Trying to make the other person feel better for your own sake but ignoring the feelings involved.

'You will cope with it, I'm sure you will.'
'You're just going through a bad patch, you'll come out of it.'
'Don't take it so personally, it happens to all of us at some time.'

11 Diagnosing

Playing the amateur psychologist and labelling the other person.

'You are suffering from an inferiority complex.'
'I do think you're being very paranoid about this.'
'You really are quite neurotic.'

12 Over-interpreting

Trying to explain away the other person's problems and concerns without due sensitivity to how they might view those problems.

'The reason you don't enter into the spirit of things in the staffroom is because you think we are all beneath you.'
'Your lack of energy is more to do with not getting promotion than with extra work.'

'If you had children of your own you would know what it's like for some of these parents.'

13 Distracting

Confusing the issue by changing the subject.

> 'Well, let's not dwell on that, shall we?'
> 'Ah, I'd rather leave that for another time.'
> 'Oh by the way did I tell you I had sent off for those course details you asked about?'

14 Faking attention

Pretending to show interest and concern where there is none.

> 'Really?'
> 'Oh, I know.'
> 'Yes, I'm sure you have.'

15 Time pressures

Indicating that your time is limited.

> 'I'm expecting a visitor in a few minutes.'
> 'I've got to be at County Hall in half an hour.'
> 'I can give you a few minutes.'

This is not to suggest that these strategies in themselves are always wrong or always to be avoided in interpersonal communication. Clearly, many of them have an important place in our day to day dealings with the people we live and work with. However, used in those specific contexts where it is necessary to encourage disclosure, openness and honesty then it is likely that they will be counter productive, creating a sense of frustration, insecurity and mistrust in the other person.

Conclusion

This chapter has been concerned with the importance of interpersonal behaviour within the context of appraisal and staff development. By way of summary the following diagram attempts to relate these to two sets of concerns. Firstly an awareness of and concern for the factors relating to human growth and development which need form the basis of management and leadership, and secondly the behaviours and skills themselves.

Personal and professional relationships

```
┌─────────────────────────────────────────────────────────────┐
│      FACTORS RELATING TO HUMAN GROWTH AND DEVELOPMENT        │
└─────────────────────────────────────────────────────────────┘
                    │
           ┌────────────────────┐
           │  Human potential   │
           │  Self concept      │
           │  Motivation        │
           │  Empowerment       │
           │  Locus of control  │
           └────────────────────┘
                    │
                    ▼
              ╭──────────────╮
              │ PROFESSIONAL │
              │ DEVELOPMENT  │
              ╰──────────────╯
                    ▲
           ┌────────────────────┐
           │  Listening         │
           │  Empathy           │
           │  Warmth            │
           │  Genuineness       │
           │  Feedback          │
           └────────────────────┘
        Non-verbal communication
    Avoidance of barriers to communication

┌─────────────────────────────────────────────────────────────┐
│    INTERPERSONAL SKILLS FOR MANAGEMENT AND LEADERSHIP        │
└─────────────────────────────────────────────────────────────┘
```

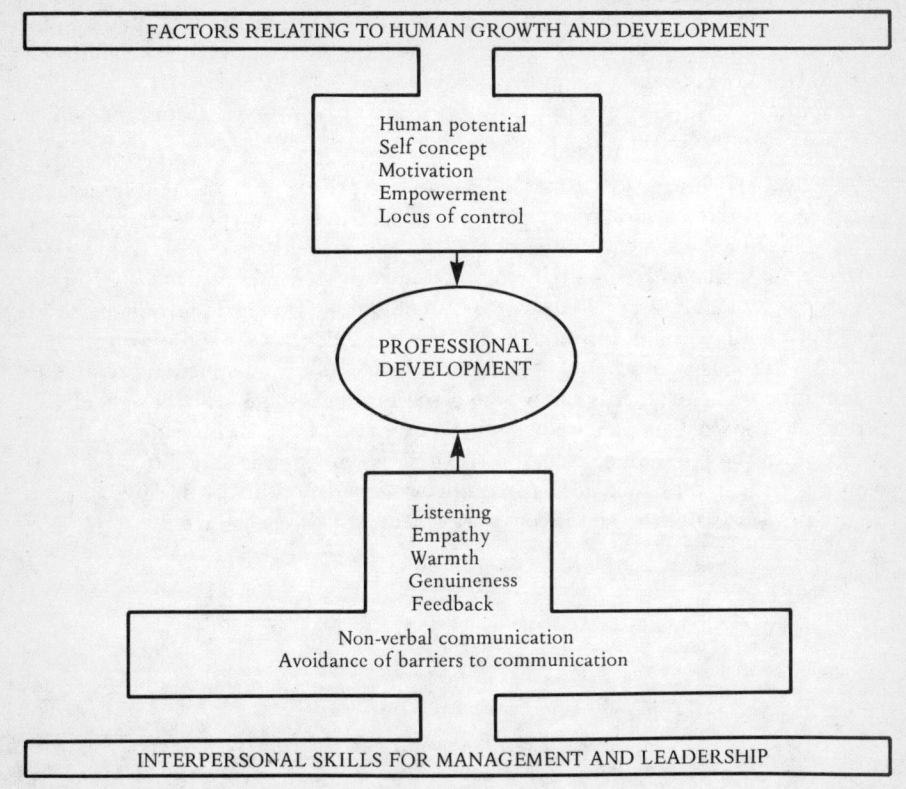

Figure 7.3: Factors relating to human growth and development

Perhaps the final attempt to relate these various factors of communications and relationships to the appraisal work of the school as a whole can best be achieved by reference to the concept of the self renewing school. (Murgatroyd 1985). The self renewing school is one that sees itself in a constant state of change and development, ever open to new challenges and opportunities. Such a school has a number of key characteristics:

1 It thrives on human interactions.
2 There is a high degree of organisational awareness and high self-awareness among the individual members of the teaching team.
3 There is a climate of interpersonal warmth, a sense of sharing a task and enjoying the process of working together.
4 Those in leadership positions pay particular attention to the needs and motivation of the team as a whole and to its individual members.
5 There is a high level of genuineness. Status differences are minimised and there is little attempt to hide behind roles.
6 There is a healthy capacity for confrontation, for facing up to difficulties, particularly interpersonal ones, and for dealing with them in an open and honest way.

7 Individual team members show a high capacity for self disclosure. They are free and caring in their encouragement of others and open and honest about their own particular weaknesses and shortcomings.
8 Communications and relationships have a quality of intimacy about them which makes for a high sense of purpose and a spirit of endeavour.

The self renewing school is not an easy one to achieve. For those in leadership positions it requires courageous example setting, patience and perseverance. From all members of the team it demands an attention to self-awareness, an ability to listen to colleagues with empathy, genuiness and warmth and a capacity to take risks and learn from apparently unsuccessful outcomes. The introduction of more systematic approaches to appraisal and professional development could do much to shift the emphasis in school management from tasks and functions to the all important human elements upon which the ultimate success of the school will depend. In the final chapter we provide an example of this by offering a practical approach to the building of a whole school policy on appraisal. It shows both the sequence of activities that need to be undertaken if a policy is to develop from existing practice and the specific activities necessary at each stage.

8 Building a school policy

The chapter is built on a developmental model which sets policy making within a planned sequence of operations. The model is not definitive, it is offered as one possible approach. Although it is systematic and sequential it should not be followed slavishly but used as a basis for planning. It will benefit from being refined, modified and expanded.

Implicit in the design of the model are a number of key principles:

1 *Policy making is best achieved by following a systematic approach.*
2 *The systematic approach demands the sequential undertaking of key processes.*
3 *An appropriate time scale for the work needs to be allocated.*
4 *Policy making is best achieved through the involvement and active participation of all the staff.*
5 *Leadership in policy making is seen as a function of the staff team rather than as a function of a key individual. All staff should be seen as co-managers in the policy making process.*
6 *For planned change to be successful full note needs to be taken of Chapter 2.*

Participation and involvement

If a policy of appraisal and professional development is to satisfy the hopes and expectations raised for it by staff, it is essential that they are fully involved in the process of making and implementing it. While the headteacher will occupy a key role in facilitating the critical path through the various phases of the policy making operation, all staff need to feel a sense of ownership and commitment to the process and its anticipated end products. Good teamwork results when there is a high capacity to distinguish between the task skills of policy making and the process skills which facilitate them.

Task skills

These are the practical, professional, technical and operational skills required to undertake and complete tasks. Such skills provide individuals with the ability to deal successfully with a wide range of activities within their professional environment. Included in them would be:

- Planning;
- Creating;
- Organising;
- Evaluating;
- Designing.

Process skills

These are the skills which are employed when individuals come together in a working group. Here the emphasis is on co-operation, human interaction and participative decision making.

A variety of processes are at work when people set out to work together and a good team is one which is particularly aware of the following:

- Thoughts – the way group members think and the different patterning of their thoughts;
- Feelings – how group members feel about the task, each other and the process of working together;
- Values – the ways group members regard each other, their attitudes, beliefs and judgements which bear upon the task;
- Behaviours – the different ways group members act and the skills they employ.

Attention to the process of skills often enables the vital task of the group to be released. Awareness of and attention to the process of working together can affect the outcomes and results in a very positive way. When there is a preoccupation with the task it can be difficult to notice that poor process is inhibiting group cohesion and effectiveness. Groups which are concerned to develop good working processes often ask one or two members to act as process observers. Their job is to provide feedback to the group on the processes which seem to be either facilitating or inhibiting progress. Such information enables a working group to build on their strengths and to minimise their weaknesses.

The staffing structure of a primary school can sometimes work to inhibit effective teamwork. It is not uncommon to find in a school of around 200 pupils a staffing structure with a wide variety of status levels, see Figure 8.1.

Within a management team of eight, separated in this hierarchical way there are a number of potential strains and tensions:

1. The problem of equitable responsibility;
2. The difficulty of creating a sense of shared responsibility for the management of the school;
3. The issue of salary differentials;

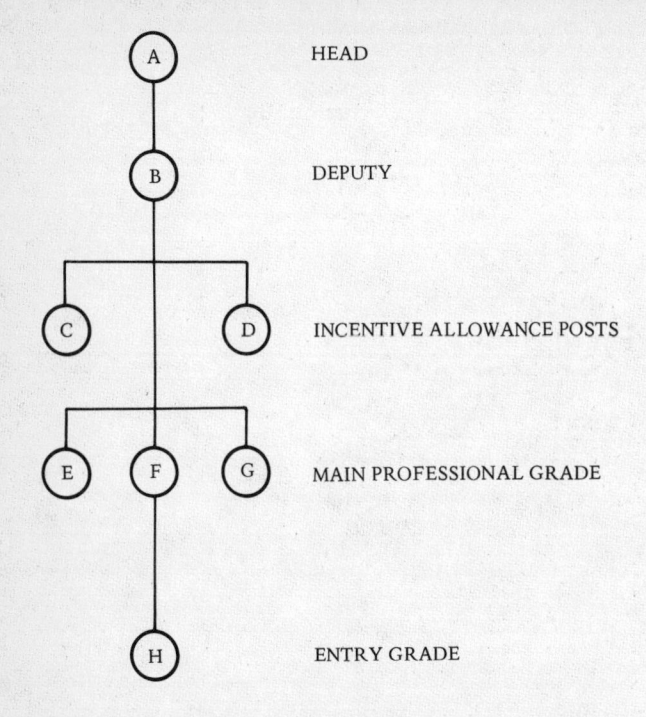

```
    A ─── HEAD

    B ─── DEPUTY

 C     D ─── INCENTIVE ALLOWANCE POSTS

E  F  G ─── MAIN PROFESSIONAL GRADE

    H ─── ENTRY GRADE
```

Figure 8.1: Hierarchical structure

4 The question of accountability.

Schools where effective teamwork operates have usually succeeded in suspending the traditional hierarchical structure in favour of a more collegial approach. This can be done by developing participative structures for decision making and policy formation and by undertaking in-service training in the skills and techniques of effective groupwork.

During the course of a school year the staff of a school will undertake a wide range of planning, policy making, curriculum development and evaluation activities. Instead of always tackling these through the whole staff team, the bulk of the work can be undertaken by smaller teams or task groups. An alternative to the structure illustrated above could be a system based on a variety of groupings, see Figure 8.2. Some of these task groups may be quite short lived, maybe existing for half a term or even less. Others may be of longer duration and the membership of them may change from time to time. Rather than undertaking their work for the headteacher task groups work on behalf of the whole staff team. They will make periodic reports to the full staff and receive recommendations, observations, responses and instructions.

Within the working groups, status differentials can be minimised and each

150 *Appraisal and professional development in the primary school*

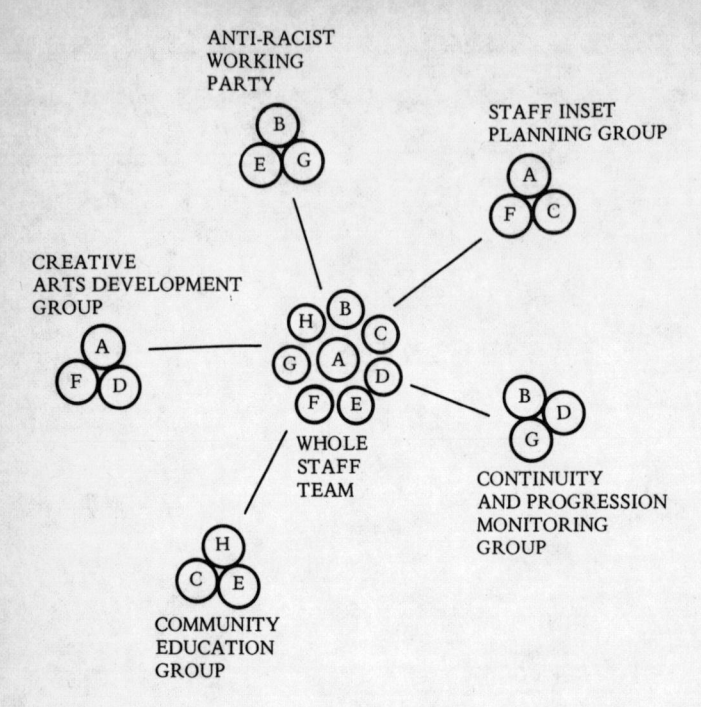

Figure 8.2: Collegial structure

member of staff encouraged to contribute according to their experience and skill. There are many benefits to be accrued from a highly dynamic and participative structure such as this:

1 It maximises staff expertise and experience.
2 It involves all staff in key management activities.
3 It achieves a higher work rate.
4 It removes the frustrations often experienced when decision making is attempted in too large a group.
5 It develops new skills and expertise.
6 It facilitates professional development.
7 It increases enjoyment and commitment.
8 It recognises the importance of the four key motivators:
    affiliation
    appreciation
    achievement
    influence.
9 It makes better use of time.
10 It allows quick responses to new problems.

Working methods and techniques

The following suggestions are offered as ways of improving teamwork within task groups, and for the whole staff team.

Preparatory documents

These are papers which help individuals to become familiar with the background and purposes of task group activity. They are best conceived as brief but explicit statements which offer:

- background information;
- briefing instructions;
- key questions;
- practical examples;
- success criteria;
- resource implications.

Group techniques

Brainstorming - listing without argument or disagreement all the ideas about a specific issue which can be generated.

Index cards - generating ideas on separate cards which can then be laid out, collated and categorised. Pasted onto large sheets of paper and displayed in the staffroom these cards are an excellent way of generating and recording group work.

Making posters - a creative way of activating group energy and providing a creative outlet for thinking.

Talking in pairs - an important way to start the process of sharing ideas about issues and concerns. During the early and tentative stages of discussion it is more comfortable to locate discussion in twos. As the ideas begin to flow pairs can join up until eventually discussion is focused in the whole group.

Using observers - a useful way of monitoring the process aspect of group work. The observer can be detached from the task group or can be an active member whose additional task is to feedback observations.

Flip charts - a vital piece of equipment for effective group work. Recording thinking, ideas, possibilities, processes and decisions on flip charts helps to maintain a systematic approach and provides a visible record of the proccesses of the work.

Recording progress

It is vital that the deliberations of task groups are recorded and fed back to the whole staff. Although this can be done verbally this can be excessively demanding of time. Alternatives are:

1 display flip charts, posters, index card charts and brainstormed lists;
2 maintain a Task Group Minute Book briefly recording tasks undertaken, results

achieved, decisions taken, process implications;
3 photocopy and circulate brief summaries of group meetings;
4 store key information on computer.

The model

The model is built on a sequence of activities. The guidance provided under each of the seven phases of the developmental sequence is arranged as follows:

1 Focusing Question
  This serves to focus thinking and stimulate creativity.
2 Basic Task
  This outlines the fundamental work of the phase under consideration.
3 End Result
  This suggests the tangible outline of the phase and provides a clear target to work towards.
4 Activities
  These offer a number of tasks which will be necessary to accomplish the work of the phase. They are suggestions and some of the activities will not be necessary in some situations. Also within the specific situations of some schools there may be activities arising which are not mentioned here.

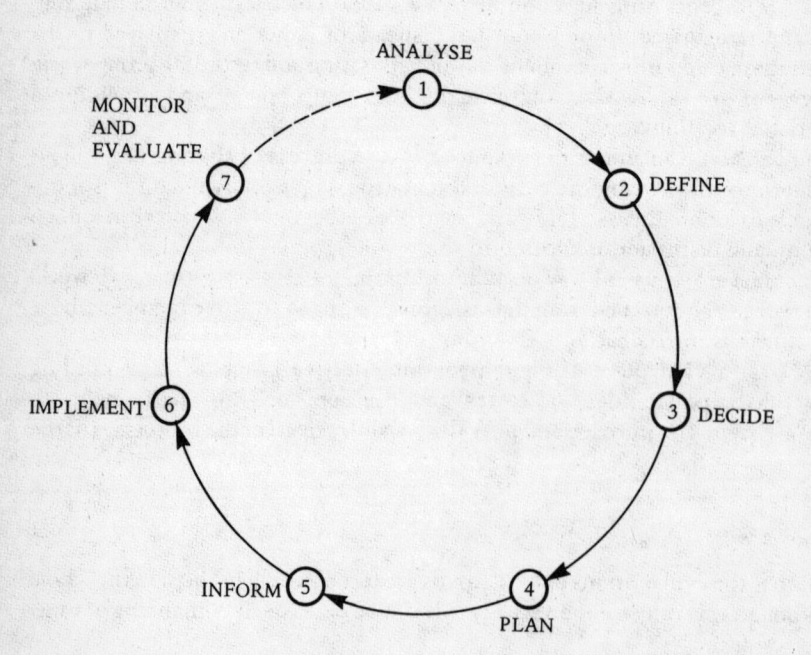

Figure 8.3: A model for building a school appraisal and professional development policy

Building a school policy

1 ANALYSE ➡

DEFINE

DECIDE

PLAN

INFORM

IMPLEMENT

EVALUATE

FOCUSING QUESTION:
What is happening now?

BASIC TASK:
An examination and analysis of existing provision and practice.

END RESULT:
A clear understanding of the range of appraisal activities currently undertaken in the school.

ACTIVITIES
1. Create an analytical framework for analysis. For example, the following would contain many areas of school life which would need to be considered for appraisal activity.
    1. pupil learning;
    2. teaching methods and techniques;
    3. classroom organisation and management;
    4. curriculum design and documentation;
    5. consultancy and coordination roles;
    6. management, leadership and decision making;
    7. school organisation and administration;
    8. resource allocation and management;
    9. pastoral care;
    10. parental involvement;
    11. staff development and career guidance;
    12. specific policies – anti-racism, anti-sexism, community education.
2. Prepare brief statements about the appraisal activities of each member of staff.
3. Reach agreement on key terms:
   Appraisal, assessment, monitoring, review, evaluation. (See Chapter 1)
4. Staff exercise to share their 'hopes and expectations' and 'fears and concerns' about appraisal.
5. Analysis and evaluation of current practice, to consider those practices which:
    1. need to be continued;
    2. need to be modified and improved;
    3. need to be discarded and/or redesigned.

ANALYSE

2   DEFINE ⇨

DECIDE

PLAN

INFORM

IMPLEMENT

EVALUATE

FOCUSING QUESTION:
What needs to be done?

BASIC TASK:
Defining what the individual and collective appraisal needs of the school are.

END RESULT:
A list of specific areas where appraisal practices need to be improved and introduced.

ACTIVITIES
1 Using the analytical framework already created, identify and locate:
   - areas for improvement and development
   - gaps and omissions in appraisal provision
2 Discuss, consider and reach agreement on the purposes and benefits of a school policy on appraisal.
3 List the specific purposes and benefits of appraisal in each of the identified areas.
4 Make available for discussion and consideration information about different appraisal methods and techniques. (See Chapters 4, 5, 6 & 7.)
5 Against each area identified for appraisal development list possible suitable methods and techniques.

ANALYSE

DEFINE

3 | DECIDE ⇨

PLAN
INFORM

IMPLEMENT

EVALUATE

FOCUSING QUESTION:
What shall we do?

BASIC TASK:
To examine and select appraisal techniques for each area of school life identified for development.

END RESULT:
A list of development areas with their specific appraisal methods.

ACTIVITIES
1 Provide briefing papers for each member of staff setting out appraisal options in each area of development.
2 Create small task groups to examine and comment upon the options in specific areas.
3 Set a timescale for these activities.
4 Submit task group proposals to the staff decision making process.
5 Make brief but explicit statements about the decisions made.

ANALYSE

DEFINE

DECIDE

4 | PLAN ⇨

INFORM

IMPLEMENT

EVALUATE

FOCUSING QUESTION:
How shall we go about making the changes?

BASIC TASK:
To create an action plan for introducing new appraisal procedures.

END RESULT:
A systematic plan showing what has to be done within the time scale decided upon.

ACTIVITIES
1 For each area to be developed establish task groups to list:
   (a) aims and objectives for appraisal;
   (b) all the activities necessary to introduce new appraisal methods and approaches;
   (c) specific roles and responsibilities necessary for the implementation;
   (d) time targets;
   (e) evaluation procedures.
2 Task groups report back on their work. Whole staff consider the nature of the task in hand in terms of:
   (a) size and scope of the innovation;
   (b) possible time constraints;
   (c) costs and resources;
   (d) other policy priorities.
3 Staff take decisions about factors listed above.
4 Task groups prepare an implementation plan showing:
   (a) time scale;
   (b) tasks and target dates;
   (c) support structures;
   (d) monitoring procedures;
   (e) roles and responsibilities;
   (f) evaluation methods.
5 Agreement on the systematic plan.

ANALYSE

DEFINE

DECIDE

PLAN

5 | INFORM ▷

IMPLEMENT

EVALUATE

FOCUSING QUESTION:
Who needs to know about the plan?

BASIC TASK:
To make formal and informal reports to
(a) governors
(b) LEA

END RESULT:
The plan approved and minuted.

ACTIVITIES
1 Undertake informal discussions and consultations with:
   (a) LEA advisers/inspectors;
   (b) colleagues in other schools.
2 Prepare summary documentation of the policy building process for presentation to governors.
3 Include proposed plan in Head's Report to Governors.
4 Discuss and explain at governor's meeting.
5 Submit plan to LEA.

ANALYSE

DEFINE

DECIDE

PLAN

INFORM

6 | IMPLEMENT ⇨

EVALUATE

FOCUSING QUESTION:
How do we manage the implementation of the plan?

BASIC TASK:
To monitor and support the introduction of new appraisal procedures.

END RESULT:
The full introduction into the school of the appraisal policy.

ACTIVITIES
1 From the overall plan prepare a critical path diagram showing the phases of the implementation. Display for all those concerned to refer to.
2 Build into the implementation regular monitoring meetings for:
   (a) individual staff;
   (b) task groups;
   (c) staff as a whole.
3 Create support structures for individuals and groups so that teaching problems are dealt with promptly.
4 Note and document:
   (a) unplanned outcomes;
   (b) staff reactions and responses;
   (c) resource implications.
5 Decide when the implementation stage is complete and formally acknowledge the fact.

ANALYSE

DEFINE

DECIDE

PLAN

INFORM

IMPLEMENT

7 | EVALUATE ⇨

FOCUSING QUESTION:
How well are new appraisal practices and procedures working?

BASIC TASK:
To evaluate the implementation of new appraisal procedures and their outcomes.

END RESULT:
Awareness and understanding of the success of the innovation. Making readjustments in the light of the evaluation.

ACTIVITIES
1 Document and respond to the outcomes of the regular implementation monitoring meetings.
2 Gather responses and reactions to the new procedures from individuals.
3 Apply the evaluation procedures agreed on at the planning stage.
4 Invite evaluation from governors and LEA advisers/inspectors.
5 Document and discuss proposals for modification and development following evaluation.

This final chapter has provided a practical way in which appraisal activities can be introduced into a school. Adopting a systematic approach like the one offered here ensures that policy making builds on existing practice, responds to teachers' hopes and expectations and facilitates whole staff involvement. Although a reasonable amount of time – two or three terms for all but the smallest schools – will need to be allocated to such a significant and important innovation, it need not demand the exclusive use of staff management time. The suggestions in the chapter about management through small task groups offer the possibility of considerable flexibility. Once implemented it is vital that practices are monitored and evaluated regularly. The self renewing school is one where experience informs development and where continual modifications and improvements can take place. Without such attention to the outcomes of a policy, both in terms of classroom life and of management activities, the long-term benefits of appraisal and professional development are unlikely to be achieved.

Bibliography

Aluth, J.A. and Belasco, J.A. (1972). 'Patterns of teacher participation in school system decision-making', *Educational Administration Quarterly* 9(1) Winter 1972.

Anning, A. (1983). 'The Three Year Itch', *Times Educational Supplement* 24 June 1983.

Argyle, M. (1975). *Bodily Communication*. London, Methuen.

Argyle, M. (1983). *The Psychology of Interpersonal Behaviour*. London, Penguin.

Argyris, C. and Schon, D.A. (1976). *Theory in Practice: Increasing Professional Effectiveness*. London, Jossey-Bass.

Aspy, D. and Roebuck, E. (1976). *A Lever Long Enough*. Washington DC, Consortium for Humanizing Education.

Auld, R. (1976). *William Tyndale Junior and Infants Schools Public Inquiry: A Report to the Inner London Education Authority*. London, ILEA.

Barker-Lunn, J. (1984). 'Junior school teachers: their methods and practices', *Educational Research*, Vol 26, No 3, November 1984.

Barnes, D. (1976). *From Communication to Curriculum*. Harmondsworth, Penguin.

Bassey, M. and Hatch N. (1979). 'A seven-category interaction analysis for infant teachers to use themselves', *Educational Research*, Vol 21 No 2.

Berg, L. (1968). *Risinghill: death of a comprehensive school*. Harmondsworth, Penguin.

Berridge, J. (1986). 'Counselling and Performance Appraisal: An L.E.A. Perspective' in Day, C. and Moore R. (eds.), *Staff Development in the Secondary School: Management Perspectives*. London, Croom Helm.

Bolam, R. (1985), in Hopkins D. (ed.) (1985) *In-service Training and Educational Development: An International Survey*. London, Croom Helm, p. 323.

Bossert, S.T. (1977). *Tasks and Social Relationships*. Cambridge, Cambridge University Press.

Bruner, J. (1961). 'The Act of Discovery', reprinted in Bruner, J.S. (1965) *On Knowing: Essays for the Left Hand*. Cambridge, Mass., Harvard University Press.

Carr, W. and Kemmis, S. (1986). *Becoming Critical: Education, Knowledge and Action Research*. London, The Falmer Press.

Clift, P. (1982). 'LEA schemes for School Self-evaluation: a Critique', *Educational Research*, Vol 24 No 4 November 1982.
Coulson, A. (1985). 'The Fear of Change'. Unpublished paper.
Croydon Education Authority (1985) *Primary Education in Croydon: A Guide for Parents*, Croydon Education Authority and the Voluntary School Authorities in Croydon, London.
Davis, E. (1981). *Teachers as Curriculum Evaluators*. London, George Allen and Unwin.
Day, C. (1986). 'Sharing Practice through Consultancy: individual and whole school staff development in a primary school' in Holly, P. and Whitehead, D. (eds.) *Collaborative Action Research*, Bulletin No 7, Cambridge, CARN Publications, Cambridge Institute of Education.
Day, C. Johnston, D. and Whitaker, P. (1985). *Managing Primary Schools: A Professional Development Approach*. London, Harper and Row.
DES. (1977). Curriculum 11-16. London, HMSO.
DES. (1978). *Primary Education in England*. London, HMSO.
DES. (1979). *Aspects of Secondary Education in England*. London, HMSO.
DES. (1981). *The School Curriculum* (Circular 6/81). London, HMSO.
DES. (1983). *The Treatment and Assessment of Probationary Teachers*. Circular 1/83. London, HMSO.
DES. (1984). *Education Observed: A Review of Published Reports by HMI*. Stanmore, DES Publications.
DES. (1985). *Better Schools*. London, HMSO.
DES. (1985). *Education Observed 3: Good Teachers*. Stanmore, DES Publications.
DES. (1985). *The Curriculum from 5-16: Curriculum Matters 2*. An HMI Series. London, HMSO.
DES. (1985). *English from 5-16: Curriculum Matters 1*. London, HMSO.
DES. (1985). *Quality in Schools: Evaluation and Appraisal*. London, HMSO.
Dean, J. (1983). *Organising Learning in the Primary School Classroom*. London, Croom Helm.
Downes, B. (1984). 'The Appraisal of Staff Development Programmes', *Education Today*, Vol 34 No 1.
Doyle, W. and Ponder, G.A. (1976). 'The Practicality Ethic in Teacher Decision Making', *Interchange*, 8 (1977).
Duke, D.L. Showers, B.K. and Imber, M. (1980). 'Teachers and shared decision-making: The costs and benefits of involvement', *Educational Administration Quarterly*, 16(1), Winter, 1980.
Easen, P. (1985). *Making School-Centred INSET Work*. Milton Keynes, The Open University in association with Croom Helm.
East Sussex Accountability Project. (1979). 'Accountability in the Middle Years of Schooling: An Analysis of Policy Options'. Brighton, University of Sussex; mimeograph in McCormick, R. (ed.) (1986). *Calling Education to Account*. London, Open University/Heinemann Educational Books.
Egan, G. (1982). *The Skilled Helper*. Monterey, California, Brooks/Cole Publishing Company.
Eisner, E. (1979). *The Educational Imagination*. West Drayton, Collier Macmillan.

Elliott, J. (1978). *The Ford Teaching Project*. CARE, University of East Anglia.
—— (1977). 'Conceptualising Relationships between Research/Evaluation Procedures and In-service Teacher Education', *British Journal of In-service Education*, Vol 4 Nos 1 and 2.
—— (1978). *Who Should Monitor Performance in Schools?* Mimeo. Cambridge, Cambridge Institute of Education.
—— (1979). 'Accountability, Progressive Education and School-based Evaluation, in Richards, C. (ed.) *New Directions in Primary Education*. London, The Falmer Press.
—— (1981). *Action Research: A Framework for Self-evaluation in Schools*, TIQL Working Paper No 1, Mimeo. Cambridge, Cambridge Institute of Education.
—— (1982). 'Institutionalising Action Research in Schools' in Elliott, J. and Whitehead, D. (eds.) *Action Research for Professional Development and Improvement of Schooling 5*, Cambridge, CARN Publications.
—— (1983). 'Self-evaluation, professional development and accountability', London, in Galton, M. and Moon, R. *Changing Schools, Changing Curriculum*, London, Harper and Row.
—— (1984). 'Improving the Quality of Teaching through Action Research', *Forum*, Vol 26 No 3.
—— (1984). 'Implementing School-Based Action Research: Some Hypotheses', in Bell, J. *et al* (eds.) (1984). *Conducting Small-Scale Investigations in Educational Management*, London, Harper and Row.
Elliott, J. and Adelman, C. (1976). 'Innovation at the classroom level'. *Innovation the School and the Teacher (1) E203 Units 27 and 28*. Milton Keynes, The Open University Press.
Elliott, J., Bridges, D., Ebbutt, D., Gibson R. and Nias, J. (1981). *School Accountability*. London, Grant McIntyre.
Elliott-Kemp, J. and Williams, G. (1980). *The DION Handbook: Diagnosing individual and organisational needs in schools*. Sheffield, Pavic Publications.
Elliott-Kemp, J. (1982). *The Effective Teacher*. Sheffield, Pavic Publications.
Eraut, M.E. (1977). 'Strategies for Promoting Teacher Development', *British Journal of In-service Education*, Vol 4 Nos 1 and 2.
—— (1977). 'In-service Courses: their structure and functions' in Richards C. (ed.). *New Contexts for Teaching, Learning and Curriculum Studies*. Association for the Study of the Curriculum.
—— (1983). 'What is learned in in-service education and how?', *British Journal of In-service Education*, Vol 9 No 1.
—— (1986). 'Friends or Foes?' *Times Educational Supplement*, 5 September 1986.
Eraut, M.E. Barton, J. and Canning, A. (1978). *Some Teacher Perspectives on Accountability*. SSRC Working Paper (unpublished). University of Sussex School Accountability Project.
Farnsworth, S. and Garcia, K. (1985). *Developing Classroom Learning. A Handbook to support self-directed classroom inquiry*. Curriculum Development Support Service, Nottinghamshire Country Council.
Fenstermacher, G. (1983). 'How should implications of research on teaching be

used?', *The Elementary School Journal*, Vol 83 No 4.

Fletcher, C.A. (1984). 'What's New in Performance appraisal', *Personnel Management*, Vol 14, No 2.

Galton, M. *et al* (1980). *Inside the Primary Classroom*. London, Routledge and Kegan Paul.

Graham Report, The. (1985). *Those Having Torches*. Suffolk Education Department.

Gronlund, N. (1976). *Measurement and Evaluation in Teaching*. New York, Macmillan.

Hands, G. (1981). 'First catch your adviser: the INSET role of advisers' in Donoughe, C. *et al* (1981). *In-service: The Teacher and the School*. London, Kogan Page.

Harlen, W. Darwin A. Murphy, M. (1977). *Match and Mismatch: Raising Questions*. Edinburgh, Oliver and Boyd for the Schools Council.

Hartley, L. and Broadfoot, P. (1985). *Assessing Teacher Performance*, Paper presnted at BERA Annual Conference, Sheffield, August 1985.

HAY Management Consultants. (1986). Grosvenor Gardens, London SW1W 0AU.

Haydon, F. (1986). *Observation*, Occasional Paper. Leicester, Centre for Evaluation and Development in Teacher Education, University of Leicester.

Hayson, J. (1985). *Inquiring into the Teaching Process*. OISE Press.

Hendricks, G. and Hendricks, K. (1985). *Centering and the Art of Intimacy*. New Jersey, Prentice Hall.

HMSO. (1986). Education (No 2) Act. London, HMSO.

Herzberg, F. (1966). *Work and the Nature of Man*. New York, Staple Press.

Hook, C. (1981). *Studying Classrooms*. Geelong, Deakin, Deakin University Press.

Hopson, B. & Scally, M. (1981). *Lifeskills Teaching*, London, McGraw Hill.

House, E. (1972), 'The conscience of educational evaluation', *Teachers College Record* 73, 1972.

House, E.R. (1974). *The Politics of educational innovation*. Berkeley, McCutchan Publishing.

ILEA. (1983). *Keeping the School Under Review*. London, ILEA Inspectorate.

ILEA Report. (1984). *Improving Secondary Schools*, Report of the Committee on the Curriculum and Organisation of Secondary Schools.

Inskipp, F. (1985). *A Manual for Trainers*. St Leonards on Sea, Alexia Publications.

Jackson, P.W. (1968). *Life in Classrooms*. New York, Holt, Rinehart and Winston.

Kemmis, S. *et al* (1981). *The Action Research Planner*. Geelong, Deakin, Deakin University Press.

Lawton, D. (1981). 'Accountability', in Gordon, P. (ed). (1981). *The Study of the Curriculum*. Batsford Studies in Education. London, B.T. Batsford.

Lieberman, M. & Hardie, M. (1981). *Resolving Family and Other Conflicts*. Santa Cruz, Unity Press.

Lipnack, J. and Stamps, J. (1986). *The Networking Book*. London, Routledge and Kegan Paul.

McCormick, R. and James, M. (1983). *Curriculum Evaluation in Schools*. London, Croom Helm.

MacDonald, B. and Ruddock, J. (1971). 'Curriculum research and development projects: barriers to success', *British Journal of Educational Psychology*, 41.

MacDonald, B. (1973). 'Innovation and Incompetence', in Hamingson, D. (ed.), *Towards Judgement: the Publications of the Evaluation Unit of the Humanities Curriculum Project 1970-72*, Occasional Paper 1, Centre for Applied Research in Education, University of East Anglia.

Macdonald-Ross, M. (1973), 'Behavioural Objectives: A Critical Review', in Golby, M., Greenwald, J. and West, R. (eds.). (1975). *Curriculum Design*. London, Croom Helm.

Machiavelli, N. (1513) quoted in Nisbet, J. (1974). 'Bandwagon or Hearse?' in Harris A. Lawn, M. and Prescott, W. (eds.). (1975). *Curriculum Innovation*. London, Croom Helm in association with Open University Press.

McMahon, A. *et al* (1984). *Guidelines for Review and Internal Development of Schools: Primary School Handbook*. London, Longman.

McMahon, A. (1984), 'Reviewing and Developing the Curriculum: The GRIDS Project', in Skilbeck, M. (ed.). (1985). *Readings in School-based Curriculum Development*. London, Harper and Row.

Manchester LEA. (1986). *Developing our Primary Schools*. Manchester, Manchester Education Committee.

Maslow, A. (1976). *The Further Reaches of Human Nature*. London, Penguin.

Morrison, T.E., Osborne, K.W. and McDonald, N.G. (1977). 'Whose Canada? The assumptions of Canadian Studies', *Canadian Journal of Education*, Vol 2 No 1, 1977.

Murgatroyd, S. (1985). *Counselling and Helping*. London, British Psychological Society and Methuen.

Nelson-Jones, R. (1986). *Personal Responsibility Counselling and Therapy, An Integrative Approach*. London, Harper and Row.

Northamptonshire LEA. (1985). *Reflection: Evaluation of Primary Schools. An approach to self-evaluation through key questions*. Northamptonshire Education Department.

Nuttall, D. (1986), 'What can we learn from research on teaching and appraisal', in Dockrell, B., Nisbet, J., Nuttall, D., Stones, E. and Wilcox, B. (1986). *Appraising Approach*. Kendal, Cumbria, British Educational Research Association, BERA Publications.

Open University. (1980). *Curriculum in Action: Practical Classroom Evaluation* Open University Course. Block 3. Pp 234, 533. Milton Keynes, Open University Press.

Open University. (1981). *Observing Classroom Processes*, E364 Block 3 'Parkside'. Milton Keynes, Open University Press.

Peacock, A. (1987). Paper presented at Primary Headteachers Management Course, Nottingham University.

Peters, T.J. and Waterman, R.H. (1982). In *Search of Excellence: Lessons from America's Best Run Companies*. New York, Harper and Row.

Phares, J. (1976). *Locus of Control in Personality*. New Jersey, General Learning Press.

Pickover, D. (1984). 'Recognising individual needs', in Thompson, L. and Thompson, A. (1984). *What Learning Looks Like Helping Individual Teachers to*

Become More Effective, Schools Council Programme 2. London, Longman.
Plowden Report. (1967). *Children and Their Primary Schools*. London (Central Advisory Council for Education), HMSO.
Polyani, M. (1967). *The Tacit Dimension*. Garden City, New York, Doubleday.
Proppe, O. (1982). Educational evaluation as a dialectical process', *Discourse 2*, No 2, 1982.
Reid, W.A. (1978). *Thinking About the Curriculum*. London, Routledge and Kegan Paul.
Roger, I.A. and Richardson, J.A.S. (1985). *Self-evaluation for Primary Schools*. Sevenoaks, Hodder and Stoughton.
Rogers, C. (1961). *On Becoming a Person*. London, Constable.
Rotter, J.R. (1966), 'Generalised expectancies for internal versus external control of reinforcement, Psychological Monographs. 80, 1 (Entire issue). Cited in Hopson, B. and Scally, M. (1981). *Teaching Life Skills*. London, McGraw Hill.
Rotter, J.B. (1971), 'Generalized expectancies for interpersonal trust', *American Psychologist, 26*.
Schmuck, R.A. (1980), 'Interviews for strengthening the school's creativity', in Bush, T. *et al* (eds.). (1980). *Approaches to School Management*. London, Harper and Row.
Schon, D.A. (1983). *The Reflective Practitioner: How Professionals Think in Action*. London, Temple Smith Ltd.
Schools Council. (1983). *Primary Practice: Schools Council Working Paper 75*. London, Methuen Educational Ltd.
Sergiovanni, T. (1984). 'Expanding conceptions of inquiry and practice in supervision and evaluation', in *Educational Evaluation and Policy Analysis*, 6, No 4, (1984).
Shipman, M. (1974). *In-school Evaluation*. London, Heinemann Educational Books Ltd.
Simon, A. and Boyer, E.G. (eds.). (1967 and 1970). *Mirrors for Behaviour: Summary Volume*) U.S.A. Research for Better Schools Inc.
Simons, H. (1982). 'Process Evaluation in Schools', in McCormick, R. (ed.). (1982). *Calling Education to Account*. London, Heinemann Educational Books Ltd.
Simons, H. (1984). 'Ethical Principles in School Self-Evaluation', in Bell, J. *et al* (1984). *Conducting Small-Scale Investigations in Educational Management*. London, Harper and Row.
Smyth, W.J. (1984). 'Teachers as Collaborative Learners, Clinical Supervision: a state of the art review', *Journal of Education for Teaching*, Vol 10, No 1, 1984.
—— (1985). 'Developing a Critical Practice of Clinical Supervision' in *Journal of Curriculum Studies*, Vol 17, No 1, 1985.
—— (1987). 'Cinderella Syndrome: A Philisophical View Supervision as a Field of Study'. *Teachers College Record*, Summer, 1987.
Stake, R.E. (1969). 'Language Rationality and Assessment', in Beatty, W.H. (ed.). *Improving Educational Assessment and an Inventory of Measures of Affective Behaviour*. Washington, DC, Association for Supervision and Curriculum Development.
Stenhouse, L.A. (1975). *An Introduction to Curriculum Research and Development*.

London, Heinemann Educational Books Ltd.
Stenhouse, L. (1979). *What is action-research?* mimeograph. CARE, University of East Anglia.
—— (1983). 'Research as a basis for teaching', in Stenhouse, L. (1983) *Authority, Education and Emancipation*. London, Heinemann Educational Books Ltd.
Stiggins, R.J. and Bridgeford, N.J. (1984). 'Performance Assessment for Teacher Development'. Centre for Performance Assessment, Northwest Regional Educational Laboratory, 300 SW, Sixth Avenue, Portland, Oregon, January 1984, in *The Graham Report* (1985) op cit.
Strake, R.E. (1967). 'The Countenance of Educational Evaluation', *Teachers College Record*, LXVIII-7 April 1967.
Stubbs, M. (1976). *Language, Schools and Classrooms*. London, Methuen.
Sutton, C. (1981). *Communicating in the Classroom*. Sevenoaks, Hodder and Stoughton.
Taylor Report. (1977). *A New Partnership for Our Schools*. London, HMSO.
Taylor, W. (1985). 'The task of the school and the task of the teacher'. Paper 1 for DES Conference on 'Better Schools: evaluation and appraisal', Birmingham, 1985.
Thomson, A. (1984). 'The Use of Video as an Observation Tool', in Thomson, L. and Thomson A. (1984) op cit.
Thomson, L. and Thomson, A. (1984). *What Learning Looks Like: Helping Individual Teachers to Become More Effective*, Schools Council Programme 2. London, Longman.
Toffler, A. (1971). *Future Shock*. London, Pan Books.
Turner, G. and Clift, P. (1985). 'Teachers' Perceptions of a Voluntary LEA scheme for School Evaluation', *Educational Research*, Vol 27, No 2.
Walker, R. (1985). *Doing Research: A Handbook for Teachers*. London, Methuen.
Walker, R. and Adelman, C. (1975). *A Guide to Classroom Observation*. London, Methuen.
Warnock Report, The (1978). *The Education of the Handicapped*. London, HMSO.
White, J. (1981). 'Enigmatic Guidelines', in White, J. *et al* (1981). *No, Minister: a critique of the DES Paper 'The School Curriculum'*, Bedford Way Paper 4. London. University of London Institute of Education.
Whitehead, A. (1981). 'An Introduction' in Bonham, W.B. *Business Adrift*. Maidenhead, McGraw-Hill.
Wilcox, B. (1986). 'Contexts and Issues' in Dockrell, B. *et al* (1986). *Appraising Appraisal*. British Educational Research Association BERA Publications.
Withall, J. and Wood, F. (1979) 'Taking the threat out of classroom observation and feedback', *Journal of Teacher Eduation*, 30 Jan-Feb 1979.
Yinger, R. (1979). 'Routines in teacher planning', *Theory in Practice*, XVIII.
Zaltman, G. Florio, D. and Sikorski, L. (1977). *Dynamic Educational Change*. New York, Macmillan.

Index

accountability, 1, 2, 12, 13, 14, 53, 65, 81, 149
achievement, 21, 128
action plan, 115
action research, 28, 65-70, 109-113
actualizing tendency, 126
Adleman, C., 97, 106
advisers/inspectors, 4, 37, 40, 52, 58, 70, 71, 75, 157, 159
advising, 142
advisory service, 4, 25
affiliation, 21
aggressive behaviour, 142
Aluth, J., 22
anecdotal records, 82, 93
Anning, A., 38
answerability, 14
appearance, 140-141
appraisal,
  aims and objectives, 7
  building a school policy, 147-160
  climate, 11, 12
  comment form, 120-3
  context, 1-12
  definitions, 5
  elements, 7-11
  follow-up, 124
  from above, 70-3
  from below, 75-6
  interview, 7, 8, 11, 16, 22, 28, 114-124, 126, 132-5, 137
  LEA role, 5-7, 116
  legislation, 9-11
  peer, 7, 8, 12, 52, 73-6
  process, 118-123
  purposes of, 7, 13-18
  school context, 11-12
  self, 12, 16-19, 52-78, 80, 118
appreciation, 21, 128
APU, 2
Argyle, M., 139, 141
Argyris, C., 20, 81
Aspy, D., 131, 132
assessment, 5
assumptions, 20, 35-7, 41
attending, 28, 132, 133
attitudes, 18, 19, 34-8, 128
audio recording, 84
Auld, R., 2
authentic behaviour, 42, 43
awareness, 32-51, 124, 127, 146

Barker-Lunn, J., 3, 32, 99
Barnes, D., 103, 105, 107
barriers to communication 141-4
Barton, J., 19
Bassey, M., 104
behavioural objectives, 77, 78
Belasco, J.A., 22
beliefs, 35, 36, 128
belonging, 128
Berg. L., 2
Berridge, J., 71
Black Papers, 2
blaming, 142
bodily contact, 140
bodily posture, 140
Bolam, R., 25
Bossert, S.T., 97
Bridgford, N.J., 70

Broadfoot, P., 15
Bruner, J. 105
burden of incompetence, 23

Callaghan, J., 1, 2
Canning, A., 19
career development, 12, 14, 28, 55, 72, 119, 122
Carr, W., 66
change, 12, 13-31, 32, 33, 35, 39, 44, 47, 62, 125
checklists, 53-6, 107, 108
classroom inquiry, 79-113
classroom observation, 7, 16, 71, 72, 79-113
Clift, P., 11, 54
climate, 11, 12, 46, 61, 126, 129, 145
clothes, 140
collegial staffing structure, 149, 150
collegiality, 73
co-management, 126, 147
commitment, 42, 43, 60, 72
communications, 42, 61, 119, 125-146
community, 2, 4, 8, 12, 53, 56, 72, 122
community education, 35, 135
conditions of service, 4
confidentiality, 11, 12, 28, 70
conflict, 35, 43
confrontation, 42, 43, 145
congruence, 127
connoisseurship, 19, 81
core curriculum, 3
Coulson, A., 45
counselling skills, 136-7
courage, 127
credibility, 28
Croydon LEA, 6, 77
culture of the school, 41
Cumbria LEA, 6
curriculum documents, 33, 76
Curriculum in Action, 87, 88

Davis, E., 62
Day, C., 16, 46, 109
Dean, J., 73, 77
decentralisation, 49
definitions, 5, 153
denying feelings, 142
Department of Education and Science, 2, 3, 4, 5, 6, 16, 20, 70, 76, 79, 98
diagnosing, 143
DION, 59
directing, 141

disciplined intuition, 23
disclosure, 24, 26, 27, 137-8, 145
distracting, 144
double loop learning, 20, 23, 80
Downes, B., 72
Doyle, W., 24, 26, 27
Duke, D.L., 22

Eason, P., 62
East Sussex Accountability Project, 14
Education (No. 2) Act, 1986, 9, 12
Egan, G., 27, 28, 30
Eisner, E., 19, 77, 81
Elliott, J., 15, 21, 24, 25, 53, 65, 66, 68, 69, 80, 106
Elliott-Kemp, J., 59, 60, 127
empathy, 127, 135-6, 146
empowerment, 30, 31, 129-130
English, from 5-16
   Curriculum Matters, 1, 131
Eraut, M.E., 16, 17, 19, 20, 23
evaluation, 5, 79
evaluation framework, 95

facial expression, 139
faking attention, 144
Farnsworth, S., 88, 92
feedback, 11, 12, 26, 27, 76, 81, 119, 137, 138
feelings, 18, 30, 45, 125, 148
Fenstermacher, G., 19
Fletcher, C.A., 16
fly eyed, 50
following, 132, 133
Ford Project, 106
formative evaluation, 70
future, 48, 49
fuzziness, 50

Galton, M., 32
Garcia, K., 88, 92
gaze, 140
generalised ideology, 33
genuineness, 137, 145, 146
gestures, 140
governors, 8, 34, 38, 40, 53, 76, 157, 159
Graham Report, The, 5, 6, 13, 14, 15, 16, 17, 22, 73, 79
great debate, the, 1, 5
GRIDS, 56-9, 62
Gronlund, N., 93, 95
groupwork, 89, 105

Hands, G., 27
Hardie, M., 130
Harlen, W., 80
Hartley, L., 15
Hatch, N., 104
HAY Consultants, 17
Hadon, F., 99, 101, 103
Haysom, J., 106
headship and change, 45, 46
headteachers, 4, 5, 8, 11, 12, 13, 14, 15, 27, 32, 38, 39, 40, 47, 54, 55, 61, 64, 70, 78, 80, 115, 116, 126, 136, 137, 147, 157
helping, 27, 28, 30
Hendricks, G., 136
Hendricks, K., 136
Her Majesty's Inspectors, 2, 4, 32, 41, 72, 75, 131, 132
Herzberg, F., 128
hierarchical staffing structure, 149
holons, 49
Hook, C., 82, 107
Hopson, B., 129
House, E., 14, 22
human potential, 125–7

iceberg theory, 44, 46, 127
ideals, 35, 36
ideologies, 35–8
ILEA, 21, 53
Imber, M., 22
induction, 55
influence, 21, 128
Ingham, H., 137, 138
INSET, 4, 12, 26, 27, 55, 118, 119, 122
Inskipp, F., 136
institutional analysis, 35
interactions, 42, 125
interrogating, 143
interviews with pupils, 82
intimacy, 42, 43
involvement, 27, 39, 128, 147–151

Jackson, P.W., 77
James, M., 19, 66
Jo-Hari Window, 137, 138
job descriptions, 39, 40, 119
Johnston, D., 16, 46
judging, 142

Keeping the School Under Review, 53
Kemmis, S., 66, 67

Lawton, D., 2
LEAs 1, 2, 3, 4, 8, 11, 12, 14, 15, 18, 20, 23, 30, 34, 38, 40, 49, 52, 53, 54, 57, 70, 76, 77, 118, 119, 124, 157
leadership, 13, 27, 28, 30, 39, 46–8, 50, 61, 72, 122, 130, 145, 146, 147
legislation, 9–11, 15, 20, 53
lesson profile, 97
levels, 49
Lieberman, M., 130
Lipnack, J., 49
listening, 28, 80, 118, 119, 131–6, 146
locus of control, 130
Luft, J., 137, 138

Macdonald, B., 22, 23
Macdonald-Ross, M., 77
Machiavelli, N., 44
management by walking about, 46
Manchester LEA, 63, 64
Manpower Services Commission, 3
Maslow, A., 126
McCormick, R., 19, 66, 109
McMahon, A., 57, 58
'me and we', 51
media, 1, 10, 114
monitoring, 80
moralising, 142
Morrison, T.E., 22
motivation, 21, 22, 27, 42, 43, 72, 124, 128, 145, 150
Murgatroyd, S., 137, 145

Nelson-Jones, R., 141
networking, 49
Newcastle upon Tyne LEA, 6
nodes and links, 50
non verbal communication, 139–141
Northants LEA, 54
Nuttall, D., 7

observation schedules, 84
openness, 11, 27, 42, 43, 53, 132
optimism, 127
ORACLE, 32
organisational awareness, 32–51, 145
organisational boundaries, 34
organisational environment, 33
organisational model, 33–5, 46
Osborne, K.W., 22
over interpreting, 143
ownership, 12, 22, 79, 128

Index

parents, 2, 4, 53, 56, 72, 76, 122
participation, 15, 21, 22, 39, 126, 147–151
payment by results, 10
Peacock, A., 60
permanency of change, 47
person centred, 33, 126, 128
perspectives consciousness, 50
Peters, T.J., 46, 51, 53
Phares, J., 130
photographs, 85
Pickover, D., 112
Plowden Report, The, 99
Polyani, M., 19
polycephalous, 50
Ponder, G.A., 24, 26, 27
positive regard, 127
power, 28
power and authority, 34, 35, 38–41, 126
process skills, 147, 148–150
professional associations, 12, 15
professionalism, 1, 11, 15, 30, 37, 44
promoting self respect, 47
Proppe, O., 30
psychological climate, 35, 126
pupil 'wait' time, 106
pupil outcomes and teacher performance, 76–8
pupil pursuit, 99–103

questionnaires, 83

reassuring, 143
Reid, W.A., 25
reflecting, 132, 133
reflection, 22, 23, 30, 80, 81
relationships, 11, 27, 28, 33, 34, 36, 41–4, 49, 50, 61, 72, 121, 125–146
resistance to change, 23–6, 39, 45
responsibility, 14
review, 5
Richardson, J.A.S., 81
Risinghill Comprehensive School, 2
risk taking, 48, 146
ritual behaviour, 41
Roebuck, E., 131, 132
Roger, I.A., 81, 136, 137
Rogers, C., 126
roles and responsibilities, 40, 41
Rotter, J., 28, 130
Rowe, M.B., 106
Ruddock, J., 23

Salford LEA, 6

Scally, M., 129
Schon, D.A., 20, 21, 25, 81
school brochures, 33
Schools Curriculum Development Committee, 3
school documents, 38
school focused INSET, 55
school review, 52–78
Schools Council, 3, 57, 60, 61
Schools Council Working Paper No. 75, 60
Schools Examination Council, 3
Secretary of State for Education, 3, 6, 9, 10, 12
self awareness, 127, 137, 145
self concept, 127–8
self confidence, 24, 25
self confrontation, 25
self esteem, 24, 27, 74
self monitoring teacher, 63–70
self renewing school, 145, 146
Sergiovanni, T., 19
Shipman, M., 79
Showers, B.K., 22
Simon, A., 107
Simons, H., 22, 53
simultaneous loose/tight properties, 51
single loop learning, 20, 80
Smyth, W.J., 21, 25, 26, 31, 87
spacial behaviour, 140
Stake, R.E., 95, 96
Stamps, J., 49
stealing the agenda, 143
Stenhouse, L., 25, 52, 66
Stiggins, R.J., 70
Stubbs, M., 104
Suffolk LEA, 6, 9
summarising, 120
summative evaluation, 70
Surrey LEA, 11
Sutton, C., 106
systems theory, 50

task skills, 147, 148
Taylor, W., 79
Taylor Report, The, 2, 3
teacher learning and change, 12, 13–31, 73
teacher led discussions, 106
teacher-pupil interaction, 103–108
teacher review, 52–78
teachers with special responsibility, 55
teamwork, 42, 125, 147, 148, 149
temporary teams, 46
Thompson, A., 74, 109

Thompson, L., 109
time pressures, 144
Toffler, A., 48, 49
tolerance of ambiguity, 47
triangulation, 92
trust, 11, 27, 28, 115, 127
Turner, G., 11, 54

values systems, 35, 36
values, 17, 18, 34, 36, 51, 68, 127, 148
values and attitudes, 34–8, 125
video recording, 85, 108
voice, 141

Walker, R., 82, 97, 107

warmth, 42, 137, 146
Warnock Report, The, 3
Waterman, R.H., 46, 51, 53
Whitaker, P., 16, 46
White, J., 3
Whitehead, A., 48
Wilcox, B., 7
will to achieve, 127
William Tyndale Primary School, The, 2
Williams, G., 59, 60
Withall, J., 26
Wood, F., 26

Yinger, R., 20

Zaltman, G., 81

This book is to be returned on or before
the last date stamped below.

19 DEC 1988

LIBREX—